simply
Appetizers

Editor: Jonathan Silverman
Layout and typesetting: Patty Holden
Cover: Patty Holden
Copy editing: Elizabeth Penn
Index preparation: Jonathan Silverman
Recipe consultation: Kelsey Lane

Printed in China

ISBN 1-930603-61-4

Nutritional analysis computations
are approximate.

Table of Contents

Basics   6

Cold Appetizers   9

Warm Appetizers   69

Index   126

The World of Appetizers

Appetizers, finger foods, starters, hors d'oeuvres: whatever name you give them, they are the food that kicks off every great feast. When you're cooking for your next meal, whether it is for yourself, the family, or a party, appetizers are always you and your guests' first taste of the food to come. So, if it is a neighborhood barbecue, holiday gathering, or just a night in front of the TV, it is important to start it off right and get those taste buds working. Not only are these delightful dishes often as anticipated as the entrees to follow, they can also be colorful, creative, and easier than you ever imagined.

This book will treat you to small, elegant dishes from all over the world. Ranging from European to Mediterranean, Hispanic to Asian, this broad range of recipes is quick and easy both to shop for and to make; most of the ingredients are very common—and allow you to create extraordinary snacks and small meals.

Basics

The most important ingredient in appetizers is imagination. The boundaries that may exist when preparing and cooking main courses are very rarely a problem when you are putting together appetizers. Because you and your guests will only be having a small portion of each appetizer, strong flavors and exotic colors are possible. When you want to get elaborate with presentation, these first courses are a perfect place to start because you need not make too much. Creativity comes from two sources, your ingredients and your presentation tools.

Ingredients

Choose ingredients that are fresh, colorful, and even a bit exotic. Many appetizer dishes involve no cooking so the fish, cheeses, herbs, and vegetables you select must be fresh and high quality. Remember when planning a meal to think about what produce is in season and try to work those items into your menu. If you are still not sure what to buy, ask your grocer. Perfect, vine-ripened tomatoes can make your mozzarella skewers mouth-watering, and fresh tuna will make sushi so tasty you may not even need a dipping sauce.

Tools

The photo on the right shows just a few of the things that can turn an ordinary snack into an appetizer fit for kings and queens. Muffin tins make things easier for many of your phyllo cups and short breads. They create uniformity in shape and size and allow you to make filled cups that come out perfect every time. Baking molds are the ideal way to make bases for canapés, tartlets, and filled desserts. These metal tools are very easy to use and come in a wide variety of shapes and sizes. Cookie cutters are not just for cookie dough when it comes to making appetizers. They are a great way to cut vegetables like carrots, cucumbers, zucchini, and even bell peppers into fun shapes that stay close to perfect if you are serving cold appetizers.

Cold Appetizers

Cold appetizers mean crisp, fresh, colorful, and delicious food. When herbs, fruits, and vegetables are served fresh, they maintain their natural color, texture, and nutrients. You can take advantage of this by choosing high quality foods and serving them soon after getting them home from the store. It also means that layering crisp vegetables and cheeses can be more fun than ever. These recipes are based on various types of bread, cheese, fish, and meats, with a few fresh herbs and tangy sauces to bring it all together.

Assorted Skewers

Appetizers using ham, sausage, or cheese are great because they're quick and easy to make. There are a few things you need to take into account to ensure that you and your guests get the right amount of food.

For a cheese platter, count on 3½ ounces of cheese per serving and include a little something for everyone, i.e., both mild and spicy cheeses with varying fat contents, hard and soft cheese, goat, and blue cheese. When sliced or cubed, cheese dries out quickly and should therefore be covered with plastic wrap until it's served. You can also cut sausage into cubes or slices. Ham, whether smoked, cooked, or dried is usually presented in thin slices and, like sausage, refrigerated and wrapped in plastic wrap until it is served.

Serves 4:
For the Salami and Cheese Skewers:
7 ounces hard salami
1 red bell pepper
7 ounces Gouda
16 pitted black olives
2 sage leaves cut into strips
For the Cheese-Tomato Skewers:
7 ounces Gouda
8 cherry tomatoes
16 pimento stuffed green olives
16 small basil leaves
Coarsely ground black pepper
Plus:
8 wooden skewers about 8 inches long

Prep time: 20 minutes
Per serving approx: 454 calories
31 g protein/37 g fat/7 g carbohydrates

For the salami skewers, remove skin from salami and cut into ¾-inch cubes.

Rinse bell pepper, remove stem, seeds, and white flesh, and cut pepper into bite-size pieces. Cut cheese into cubes. Alternately place pieces of salami, cheese, bell pepper, and olives on 4 skewers and sprinkle with sage leaf strips.

For the tomato skewers, cut cheese into cubes. Rinse tomatoes. Alternately place olives, cheese, basil leaves, and cherry tomatoes on 4 skewers and sprinkle with coarse pepper.

Mild Gouda on skewers with black or green olives combined two ways: with salami or fried chicken liver and fresh sage and with cherry tomatoes and aromatic basil.

Seasoned Nuts

Salted Almonds

4 tablespoons extra virgin olive oil
2 tablespoons butter
1¼ cups skinned almonds
¼ teaspoon chili powder
Coarse sea salt

Heat oil and butter and roast almonds over medium heat until golden. Combine chili powder and salt, add to almonds, toss over low heat, and let cool.

Crispy Sweet and Spicy Cashews

1 tablespoon sunflower oil
1¾ cups cashews
3 level tablespoons sugar
1 teaspoon salt
(preferably kosher or sea)
1½ teaspoons chili powder

Heat oil and roast cashews over medium heat while stirring. Sprinkle with sugar and salt and sauté 5 minutes while stirring until the sugar starts to melt and browns slightly. Remove from heat and continue stirring until the cashews have cooled slightly. Season with chili powder and let cool.

Spicy-Hot Nuts

2 tablespoons butter
⅓ cup brown sugar
1 small dried chili pepper without stem
1 teaspoon ground cumin
1 pinch each of cinnamon, cloves, cardamom, and salt
¾ cup skinned hazelnuts
1 cup skinned walnuts

In a pan, melt butter and then melt sugar into the butter. Crush chili pepper finely in a mortar or spice grinder. Stir chili pepper and other spices into butter. Add nuts and mix well. Spread out nuts on a baking sheet covered with parchment paper and let cool.

Cashews, almonds, macadamias, hazelnuts, and walnuts are excellent for roasting due to their low moisture content. Their mellow flavor also makes them ideal for sweet and spicy seasonings. Before roasting, however, you first have to remove the bitter, brown inner skin from some types (e.g., almonds, hazelnuts, and walnuts). To do so, pour boiling water over the nuts and let them soak briefly (almonds, walnuts) before removing the skin. Or roast them in an oven preheated to 400°F (hazelnuts), let them cool a little, and rub off the skin with a dishcloth.

Breadsticks are a perfect way to present appetizers in a unique shape. People love to snack on them, whether seasoned and topped with cheese and herbs, or wrapped with meat, cheese, or a variety of lettuce leaves. Below is a recipe for both store-bought and homemade breadsticks.

Grissini with Ham

Serves 6:
1½ cups nice arugula leaves
20 Italian breadsticks (grissini)
20 thin slices prosciutto

Rinse arugula leaves, pat dry, and remove hard stems. Wrap 2 arugula leaves around the lower third of each breadstick and then wrap with a slice of prosciutto. Arrange on a platter.

Parmesan Twists

Serves 4:
3 sheets frozen puff pastry
7 ounces hard cheese
(Parmesan or Pecorino Romano)
Freshly ground black pepper
Plus:
4 egg yolks
Caraway seeds

Place puff pastry sheets on a work surface and let thaw briefly. Grate cheese finely. Whisk egg yolks with a little cold water. Wet a baking sheet with water.

Roll out 1 puff pastry sheet onto a work surface and brush with the whisked egg yolks. Sprinkle cheese and pepper over the sheet and lay another sheet on top. Repeat this process for the remainder of the puff pastry, piling all sheets on top of one another, forming one stack.

Flatten the filled pastry sheets with a rolling pin so everything sticks together well. Using a pastry wheel, cut sheets into strips ½-inch wide. Grasp both ends of the strip and twist carefully several times and lay on the baking sheet.

Brush breadsticks with remaining egg yolks and sprinkle with caraway seeds. Bake in an oven preheated to 425°F for 10 minutes until golden brown.

Instead of caraway seeds, you can also sprinkle Parmesan breadsticks with poppy or sesame seeds.

Roquefort Cookies

Serves 4:

For the dough:
1 ½ cups all-purpose flour
1 teaspoon dry yeast
¼ cup lukewarm water
1 pinch salt
(preferably kosher or sea)
1 egg yolk
2 tablespoons butter

For the filling:
10 ounces Roquefort
¼ cup heavy cream
3 eggs
½ cup milk
Freshly grated nutmeg
Freshly ground black pepper
Salt (preferably kosher or sea)

Plus:
Butter and flour for the baking sheet

Prep time: 30 minutes
(+ 1 hour proofing time)
Per serving approx: 142 calories
7 g protein/9 g fat/9 g carbohydrates

For the dough, sift flour into a bowl and form a well in the center. Crumble yeast into the well and dissolve in the water while slowly mixing in flour from around the edges. Dust this starter dough with flour. Cover bowl with a cloth and set in a warm place away from drafts. Let the dough rise until small cracks form in the surface.

Add salt, egg yolk, and butter to the dough and knead together until smooth. Let rise until its volume has doubled.

For the filling, mash Roquefort finely with a fork and stir into the cream until smooth. Whisk eggs together with milk, add to cheese, and mix well. Season with nutmeg, pepper, and a little salt.

Flour work surface and knead dough once again. Roll dough into a rectangle and let it rise a bit more. Spread filling evenly on the dough and roll up the sheet of dough starting from the longer side. Refrigerate roll for 15–20 minutes. Grease a baking sheet and dust with flour. Slice dough roll and place slices on the baking sheet.

Bake Roquefort cookies in an oven preheated to 350°F for about 20 minutes.

Sharp tasting Roquefort and grated nutmeg are a perfect complement to one another in these yeast-dough cookies.

Palmiers

Cheese Palmiers

Serves 8:
4 sheets frozen puff pastry
1 whisked egg yolk
1 tablespoon Hungarian sweet paprika
3 ounces freshly grated Swiss cheese
Plus:
Parchment paper for the baking sheet

Prep time: 30 minutes
(+40 minutes thawing and refrigeration time)
Per serving approx: 269 calories
6 g protein/19 g fat/19 g carbohydrates

Lay out pastry sheets side by side on a well-floured work surface, let thaw for about 20 minutes, and roll out.

Brush puff pastry with whisked egg yolk, season evenly with paprika, and sprinkle with grated cheese.

Fold one of the shorter sides until the edge is in the middle of the pastry sheet. Take the new edge and fold again to the middle. Do the same on the other side of the pastry sheet. Now fold the entire sheet in half.

Cut the newly formed roll into slices ¼-inch thick, lay out on a baking sheet, and form into palmiers, rolling the two ends towards the center of the strip. Refrigerate for 20–25 minutes.

Bake palmiers in an oven preheated to 425°F for 10 minutes, turning after 5 minutes. Remove from baking sheet and place on a rack to cool.

Salami Palmiers

Serves 8:
6 sheets frozen puff pastry
1¼ pounds salami
¼ cup green olives
1 egg yolk
3 tablespoons milk
¼ cup chopped almonds
Freshly ground black pepper
Plus:
Parchment paper for the baking sheet

Prep time: 45 minutes
Per serving approx: 543 calories
16 g protein/40 g fat/29 g carbohydrates

Lay out pastry sheets side by side and let thaw briefly. Dice salami and chop olives finely. Whisk egg yolk with milk and follow the procedure shown in the photos above. Line a baking sheet with parchment paper and place palmiers on top with some space in between each. Bake in an oven preheated to 425°F for about 20 minutes until golden brown. They can be served both warm or cold.

Brush pastry sheets evenly with whisked egg yolk and milk, preferably with a pastry brush.

Roll up both short ends of the pastry sheets so they meet in the middle. Brush the seam where they join with egg yolk.

Sprinkle sheets with blackpepper. Top with diced salami, chopped olives, and almonds and press filling down slightly into the dough.

Using a sharp knife, cut rolled sheets into slices no more than ¾-inch thick.

Salami & Cheese Cream Puffs

Serves 8:
2¼ cups flour
½ cup butter
1¼ cups water
1 pinch salt (preferably kosher or sea)
7–8 eggs
5½ ounces freshly grated Gruyère
5 ounces salami
Plus:
Grease for the baking sheet

Prep time: 1 hour
Per serving approx: 417 calories
17 g protein/28 g fat/25 g carbohydrates

Sift flour into a bowl. In a pot, bring butter, water, and salt to a boil while stirring constantly. Pour all the flour into the boiling liquid at once while continuing to stir vigorously. Keep stirring until the mixture pulls away from the bottom and sides of the pot as a solid lump. Transfer to a bowl and let cool slightly.

Once cool, stir in 1 egg until it is completely incorporated into the mixture. Work in remaining eggs one by one, making sure that each one is mixed in thoroughly before adding the next. The paste should be shiny and smooth and fall easily from a spoon.

Cut cheese and salami into ¼-inch cubes. Mix both into the choux paste. Grease a baking sheet. Take spoonfuls of paste and set them on the baking sheet with enough distance between them to allow for spread while cooking.

Bake cream puffs in an oven preheated to 425°F for 20–25 minutes. Don't open the oven door during baking so they won't collapse. Serve cream puffs fresh.

If you don't want your cream puffs to be so spicy, you can replace Gruyère with the milder Swiss and substitute cooked ham for the salami.

Light choux paste serves as the base for these spicy cream puffs, which taste great alongside a cold beer or a hearty red wine.

Cracker Canapés
with Mushroom Cream

Serves 4:
25–30 mushrooms
1 ounce extra virgin olive oil
1 clove garlic
½ cup mayonnaise
1 tablespoon finely chopped parsley
Freshly ground white pepper
25 butter crackers
Plus:
Parsley for garnish

Prep time: 30 minutes
Per serving approx: 393 calories
5 g protein/25 g fat/36 g carbohydrates

Wipe mushrooms with a cloth and slice with stems. Heat oil and sauté mushrooms until soft. Remove from oil, drain, and dice all but a few slices. Peel garlic and chop finely. Stir together mayonnaise, parsley, and garlic and season with pepper. Fold this mixture into diced mushrooms.

Spread mushroom cream on crackers. Arrange mushrooms slices on top of cream and garnish with parsley.

Garlic and parsley give the mushroom cream its flavor. As an alterative, you can substitute ricotta for the mayonnaise.

Colorful Cracker Assortment

When it comes to a party, the following rule applies: anything that tastes good goes. So you can let your imagination run wild as you top and garnish your crackers. Top them with Brie, Roquefort, or Gouda cut into slices ¼-inch thick and then into squares. With Gouda, you can also cut decorative shapes using cookie cutters. Decorative cuts of salami, cooked or raw ham, turkey breast, or sausage are also great on these crispy rounds.

You can make a very simple topping from sliced hard-boiled eggs and for something more sophisticated, use shrimp, smoked fish, or even liver pâté. Garnish crackers with anchovy fillets, cherry tomatoes, walnuts, mandarin oranges, grapes, olives, maraschino cherries, mixed pickles, capers, caviar, and much more. Whatever combination you choose, you should first spread a "foundation" that not only contributes to the proper seasoning but also ensures that the topping won't slide off. In the simplest case, spread on a little mayonnaise or crème fraiche, either plain or seasoned with a little curry powder or chopped herbs. Crackers also taste great with ricotta cream or the spicy herb sour cream in the recipes below. Depending on the desired look, you can also put either one in a pastry bag with a plain or star tip and pipe it onto the crackers.

For the ricotta cream:
2½ cups ricotta
¼ cup heavy cream
½ teaspoon salt (preferably kosher or sea)
Freshly ground black pepper
For the sour cream:
¼ small onion
1 cup sour cream
2 tablespoons chopped herbs (parsley, chives, dill, chervil)

For the ricotta cream, thoroughly beat together ricotta, cream, salt, and pepper using a wire whisk or hand mixer. If the cream is still too thick to pipe easily from a pastry bag, you can mix in a little milk.

For the herb sour cream, mince onion and mix well with the other ingredients.

Colorfully topped and deliciously garnished crackers are easy, creative, and offer something for everyone!

Stuffed Figs

The combination of ripe, aromatic fruit and a wide variety of meats and cheeses provides a wealth of finger food delights. The intense sweetness of figs goes especially well with exquisite prosciutto. Make sure the figs are ripe and full of flavor as they can often become too soft or bitter. You can recognize a fresh, ripe fig by its spotless surface and slightly shiny yellow-green or blue-green-to-violet peel. After buying figs, use them up as quickly as possible because they keep in the refrigerator for no more than two days.

Serves 4:
12 large fresh figs
4 ounces thinly sliced prosciutto
For the cream:
1/2 cup mascarpone
Salt (preferably kosher or sea)
Freshly ground black pepper
Grated zest from 1/2 lemon
Plus:
48 whole, shelled pistachios

Prep time: 20 minutes
Per serving approx: 340 calories
14 g protein/14 g fat/40 g carbohydrates

Rinse figs, pat dry with paper towels, and cut into quarters. Slice prosciutto lengthwise into narrow strips and heap loosely in the center of plates or a platter. Arrange the figs around it with the pointy ends facing outward.

For the cream, stir up mascarpone and season with salt, pepper, and lemon zest. Transfer cream to a pastry bag with a star tip and pipe 1 small rosette onto each fig quarter. Garnish mascarpone rosettes with 1 pistachio nut each.

Mozzarella Skewers

Serves 4:
12 small mozzarella balls (in brine)
8 cherry tomatoes
Basil leaves
For the marinade:
4 tablespoons extra virgin olive oil
2 tablespoons white balsamic vinegar
1 dash lime juice
Coarsely ground pepper
Salt (preferably kosher or sea)
Plus:
Small wooden skewers

Prep time: 20 minutes
(+ 30 minutes refrigeration time)
Per serving approx: 277 calories
10 g protein/24 g fat/4 g carbohydrates

Drain mozzarella balls well. Rinse tomatoes and remove stems.

Mix marinade ingredients in a shallow dish. Add mozzarella and tomatoes, stir them around a little, cover, and refrigerate for 30 minutes.

Rinse basil leaves and shake dry. Alternately place mozzarella balls and cherry tomatoes on the skewers, arrange on plates, garnish with basil, and sprinkle with pepper.

Italy's national colors...the combination of mozzarella and tomatoes—
as popular as ever—is served here on skewers instead of in slices.

Canapés

Serves 4:
1 hard-boiled egg
6 cherry tomatoes
4 ounces smoked trout fillet
4 thin, cooked asparagus spears
4 slices white and dark pumpernickel bread
2 tablespoons butter
Small, rinsed lettuce leaves
12 small slices ham
For the remoulade:
½ cup mayonnaise
8–10 capers, coarsely chopped
1 teaspoon Dijon mustard
Kosher salt
Finely ground black pepper
Plus:
Dill sprigs
Parsley leaves
Coarsely cracked black pepper

Prep time: 20 minutes
Per serving approx: 318 calories
15 g protein/21 g fat/16 g carbohydrates

Peel hard-boiled egg and slice. Rinse tomatoes and cut in half or slice. Cut trout fillets on an angle into pieces about ½-inch wide. Cut asparagus spears into pieces 1½–2 inches long.

Cut bread into 1½-inch squares. Spread thinly with butter and top with lettuce leaves. Decorate with egg slices, asparagus, trout, tomato halves, and ham slices as desired.

For the remoulade, combine mayonnaise, capers, and mustard, stir well, and season to taste with salt and pepper. Pipe on small rosettes of remoulade sauce and garnish canapés with dill and parsley. Season with pepper.

Fine canapés with ham or fish. If desired, you can also toast the slices of bread before topping them.

Salmon Canapés

Serves 6:

For the short dough:

1¾ cups flour
½ cup butter
1 egg yolk
½ teaspoon salt (preferably kosher or sea)
2 tablespoons ice water

For the cheese topping:

1 cup ricotta
Salt (preferably kosher or sea)
Freshly ground black pepper
¼ cup heavy cream
1 tablespoon dill sprigs
1 tablespoon chopped chives
2 tablespoons finely chopped shallots

For the topping:

7 ounces smoked salmon,
cut into 25 pieces
Dill sprigs
Rosemary flowers

Plus:

Small square molds
(2 x 2 inches, ½-inch high)
Parchment paper

Prep time: 1 1/4 hours
(+ 30 minutes refrigeration time)
Per serving approx: 399 calories
15 g protein/26 g fat/27 g carbohydrates

For the dough, sift flour onto a work surface and make a well in the center. Cut butter into bits and place in the well along with egg yolk, salt, and water. Using a dough scraper or large knife, mix all the ingredients coarsely and chop into fine crumbs. Quickly knead into a smooth dough before the butter becomes too soft. Shape dough into a ball, wrap in plastic wrap, and refrigerate for about 30 minutes.

Roll out short dough on a floured work surface to a thickness of ¼ inch. If you want to make little "boats" as shown below, follow the directions further down: It's easiest to work two-dimensionally by rolling the dough out flat, cutting into 2-inch squares, placing the squares on a baking sheet lined with parchment paper, and baking according to directions.

MAKING BOATS:

Otherwise, place the molds side by side, grease them lightly, and lay the dough over the top. Gently press the dough down into the muffin cups and fold any extra dough over the outside of the mold. Press the dough down slightly and cut away any excess dough outside the mold.

Whether creating boats or flat canapés, pierce dough squares with a fork and bake in an oven preheated to 350°F for 10–12 minutes. Remove from oven and let cool.

For the topping, mix ricotta with seasonings and cream. Stir in herbs and shallots. Spread cheese mixture on the squares or boats, top each with 1 piece of salmon, and serve garnished with dill and rosemary flowers.

Ricotta Dumplings

Feta cheese gives these bite-size snacks a spicy flavor. If the mixture isn't salty enough for you, add a little more salt—but sparingly!

Serves 4:
5 ounces feta cheese
1¼ cups ricotta
1 tablespoon chopped parsley
Freshly ground black pepper
Salt (preferably kosher or sea)
Plus:
½ cup chopped pistachios
½ cup chopped walnuts
Whole-grain rye bread and pumpernickel rounds, toasted
Wooden toothpicks

Prep time: 20 minutes
Per serving approx: 440 calories
20 g protein/33 g fat/17g carbohydrates

Mash feta finely with a fork. Add ricotta and chopped parsley, season with salt and pepper, if desired, and mix well until you have a firm, pliable mass.

From the cheese mixture, make balls about 1 inch around. Roll cheese balls in the nuts, transfer to a platter, and refrigerate until ready to serve. Place cheese balls on bread rounds and fasten together with toothpicks.

Ricotta morsels coated with chopped pistachios or walnuts are best served with toothpicks.

Petits Fours with Cheese

When designing and filling petits fours, you should let your imagination run wild. Just make sure that the flavors of the individual components blend together well. You can also bake the short dough cups ahead of time and freeze them.

Serves 6:

For the short dough:
2 cups flour
½ cup butter
1 egg yolk
1 pinch salt
(preferably kosher or sea)
2 tablespoons water

For the cheese filling:
3½ ounces ripe Camembert
3½ ounces Stilton
¼ cup ricotta
2 ounces Cheddar
2 ounces prosciutto
1 tablespoon diced onion
½ clove garlic, squeezed
through a press
½ teaspoon hot mustard

Salt (preferably kosher or sea)
Freshly ground black pepper
1 tablespoon chopped herbs
(parsley, basil, thyme, sage)

For the ricotta filling:
¾ cup ricotta
1 teaspoon lemon juice
1 tablespoon sour cream
Salt (preferably kosher or sea)
Freshly ground black pepper
Sugar

Plus:
Various baking molds (½-inch high)

Prep time: 55 minutes
(+ 30 minutes refrigeration time)
Per serving approx: 553 calories
20 g protein/37 g fat/36 g carbohydrates

For the dough, sift flour onto a work surface and make a well in the center. Cut butter into bits and place in the well along with egg yolk, salt, and water. Using a dough scraper or large knife, mix all the ingredients coarsely, and chop into fine crumbs. Quickly knead into a smooth dough before the butter becomes too soft. Shape dough into a ball, wrap in plastic wrap, and refrigerate for about 30 minutes.

Roll out dough on a floured work surface to a thickness of ⅛–¼ inch. Place the molds side by side, grease them lightly, and lay the dough over the top. Gently press the dough down into the cups and roll over the top with a rolling pin to score the dough around the edges of the molds. Using your thumb, press the dough down into the molds so that no air bubbles remain and cut away excess dough with a knife. Pierce the dough several times with a fork and bake in an oven preheated to 350°F for 10–12 minutes without opening the oven door. Remove the molds from the oven and let cool.

For the cheese filling, cut away rind from Camembert. Mix together Camembert, Stilton, and ricotta until foamy. Cut Cheddar and ham into small cubes and add to cheese mixture along with onions and garlic. Stir in seasonings and herbs. Chill filling thoroughly. For the ricotta filling, mix together all the ingredients listed in the recipe.

Fill dough bases with the cheese or ricotta cream and garnish as desired.

Petits fours with cheese fillings: The beautiful "flower" garnish is made from choux paste (page 20) that was simply placed in a parchment bag, piped onto a lightly greased and floured baking sheet in the shape of a blossom, and baked.

Two Cheese Stuffed Vegetables

Depending on what's available, you can stuff a wide variety of vegetables or large pitted olives with creams, both spicy and otherwise. And they don't all have to be vegetables that are small by nature. You can also cut a cucumber in half lengthwise and then into pieces 1 inch long. Hollow out these pieces with a teaspoon and fill them with the ricotta. The filling also tastes great on cleaned celery sticks, and if you feel like trying something exotic, cut fresh or dried dates in half, remove the pits, and fill them with any variety of soft cheeses. In this case, however, leave out the herbs and instead spice up the cream with cayenne pepper.

Serves 4:
10 small mushrooms
1 tablespoon lemon juice
4 mild green chili peppers
12 herbed olives, pitted
8 cherry tomatoes
For the filling:
¾ cup ricotta
¾ cup sour cream
3 tablespoons half-and-half
2 cloves garlic

4 tablespoons chopped herbs (parsley, dill, chervil)
3 tablespoons freshly grated Parmesan
Salt (preferable sea or kosher)
Freshly ground white pepper
Hungarian hot paprika
Plus:
½ medium cucumber
Several lettuce leaves

Prep time: 35 minutes
Per serving approx: 340 calories
18 g protein/19 g fat/25 g carbohydrates

For the filling, thoroughly mix ricotta, sour cream, and half-and-half. Peel garlic, squeeze through a press, and add. Add herbs and Parmesan, mix well, and season with salt, pepper, and paprika. Refrigerate filling until ready to use.

Clean mushrooms, remove stems and any dark ribs inside the caps, and sprinkle caps with lemon juice. Rinse chili peppers and cut out stems from the top. Carefully remove seeds and white ribs without cutting the pepper open more than necessary. Cut open olives lengthwise. Rinse tomatoes, cut off a "lid," and remove interiors.

Place cheese mixture in a pastry bag with a star tip and fill mushrooms, chili peppers, olives, and tomatoes.

For garnish, rinse cucumber, peel in a striped pattern, cut in half crosswise, remove seeds with a sharp-edged spoon, and slice thinly.

Rinse lettuce leaves, spin dry, and tear into smaller pieces as desired. Arrange lettuce leaves and cucumber slices on a large plate or platter and then arrange stuffed vegetables decoratively on top.

Puff Pastry Squares with Cheese Filling

Serves 4:
1¼ sheets frozen puff pastry
For the mascarpone cream:
1¼ cups mascarpone
3 tablespoons heavy cream
Salt (preferably kosher or sea)
Freshly ground white pepper
Plus:
1 egg yolk whisked with a little water
Poppy seeds
White sesame seeds
Caraway seeds

Prep time: 35 minutes
(+20 minutes refrigeration time)
Per serving approx: 581 calories
15 g protein/42 g fat/35 g carbohydrates

Let puff pastry thaw. Cut sheet crosswise into 3 equally sized rectangles and use the ¼ piece as it is. Rinse a baking sheet with cold water, lay puff pastry on top, and refrigerate for 20 minutes.

Brush pastry pieces with the whisked egg yolk and alternately sprinkle with poppy, sesame, and caraway seeds. Bake in an oven preheated to 425°F for 10–15 minutes until golden. Remove from oven and let cool before cutting each piece in half crosswise.

For the mascarpone cream, mix together all ingredients, transfer to a pastry bag with a plain tip, and pipe onto the bottom halves of the puff pastry squares. Place remaining halves on top and arrange puff pastry squares on platters.

Poppy, sesame, and caraway seeds not only make these airy cheese squares visually delicious but also provide a change of taste. You can vary the mascarpone cream as desired by adding, for example, horse-radish, garlic, curry powder, or herbs.

Filled Pumpernickel

These thin, dark bread slices are filled with Tilsit cheese and a fine liver pâté. When preparing these sandwiches, make sure the cheese and pâté layers are of the same thickness because this increases the visual appeal of the filled pumpernickel and assures you and your guests of a good flavor profile. Any left over pieces of cheese can be diced and used in a salad.

Serves 4:
16 slices round pumpernickel with a 2-inch diameter
2 tablespoons softened butter
7 ounces Tilsit or Gouda
For the liver pâté:
$1/2$ cup softened butter
7 ounces fine veal liver sausage
Salt (preferably kosher or sea)
Freshly ground white pepper
Plus:
$1/4$ cup sliced almonds
$1/4$ cup chopped pistachios

Prep time: 20 minutes
Per serving approx: 612 calories
27 g protein/49 g fat/14 g carbohydrates

Spread 8 pumpernickel slices thinly with butter. Cut cheese into slices $1/4$-inch thick and cut out circles with a 2-inch diameter. Place cheese on buttered pumpernickel slices.

For the pâté, thoroughly mix butter with liver sausage. Add salt and pepper. Transfer to a pastry bag with a plain tip, pipe onto cheese slices and spread flat.

Place remaining pumpernickel slices on top of pâté and press down slightly. Spread remaining pâté all around the edges.

Roast sliced almonds in a nonstick pan without fat until golden brown. Sprinkle edges of 4 of the sandwiches with almonds and sprinkle the rest with pistachios. Chill thoroughly in the refrigerator and cut each sandwich in half with a sharp knife just before arranging on a platter.

Three Cheese Crackers

Serves 4:
20 round crackers
For the ricotta cream:
1 cup ricotta
3 tablespoons heavy cream
½ clove garlic
Salt (preferably kosher or sea)
Freshly ground white pepper
Plus:
3 ounces Roquefort
3 ounces Gouda
Small cookie cutters
1 teaspoon Hungarian sweet paprika
1 teaspoon chopped scallions

Prep time: 25 minutes
Per serving approx: 456 calories
22 g protein/28 g fat/30 g carbohydrates

For the ricotta cream, mix ricotta and cream. Peel garlic, squeeze through a press, and add. Season to taste.

Cut Roquefort and Gouda into ¼-inch slices. Then cut Roquefort into small squares and cut Gouda into various little shapes with cookie cutters.

Transfer cream to a pastry bag with a star tip and pipe onto the crackers. Dust 10 crackers with sweet paprika and top with a slice of Roquefort. Sprinkle remaining crackers with chopped scallions and top with Gouda.

Sharp Roquefort and mild Gouda. Both cheeses are excellent topping creamy ricotta and any variety of crackers.

Serves 4:
6 red cherry tomatoes
6 orange or yellow cherry tomatoes
1 teaspoon hot mustard
For the filling:
¾ cup plain cream cheese
2 tablespoons heavy cream
1 tablespoon chopped chives
Salt (preferably kosher or sea)
Freshly ground white pepper
Plus:
6 pitted black olives
1 teaspoon freshly chopped scallions

Prep time: 15 minutes
Per serving approx: 181 calories
7 g protein/11 g fat/13 g carbohydrates

Rinse tomatoes, cut off a small lid from each, and remove half the contents. Season each with a dash of hot mustard.

For the filling, thoroughly mix all the ingredients, transfer cream to a pastry bag with a star tip, and pipe into the tomatoes. Cut olives in half and place one half on top of each cream rosette. Sprinkle with scallions.

An attractive spot of color on a cheese platter that can be ready in a flash: cherry tomatoes stuffed with an herb cream cheese.

Bell Pepper-Tuna Crostini

Serves 8:
2 red bell peppers
5 scallions
1 can tuna packed in water (6 ½ ounces drained)
2 teaspoons capers
3 teaspoons lemon juice
3 tablespoons olive oil
Salt (preferably kosher or sea)
Freshly ground black pepper
Cayenne pepper
Plus:
16 thin slices of baguette

Prep time: 40 minutes
Per serving approx: 118 calories
7 g protein/6 g fat/6 g carbohydrates

Bake bell peppers in an oven preheated to 425°F until the peel blisters. Remove and place under a damp cloth or in a plastic bag so that they sweat. Remove peels, cut in half, remove stems, seeds, and white ribs, and dice.

Rinse scallions, clean, and chop finely. Drain tuna and shred with a fork. Drain capers and chop coarsely. Mix together bell peppers, scallions, tuna, capers, lemon juice, and 2 tablespoons olive oil. Season with salt, pepper, and cayenne.

Brush bread with remaining oil and bake in a toaster or on a baking sheet in an oven pre-heated to 425°F. Then spread with tuna mixture and serve.

You can also serve these crostini warm. In that case, place a slice of mozzarella on top of the tuna bell-pepper mixture and brown under a preheated broiler.

Bell pepper-tuna crostini: capers, lemon juice, and a hint of cayenne pepper provide a spicy accent.

Crostini with Chicken Livers

Serves 6:
For the liver mixture:
1 large onion
1 cup olive oil
1 pound chicken livers
3 tomatoes
5 hard-boiled eggs
Salt (preferably kosher or sea)
Freshly ground white pepper
Plus:
1 hard-boiled egg
25 thin slices of baguette
Chopped parsley for garnish

Prep time: 40 minutes
Per serving approx: 589 calories
23 g protein/45 g fat/23 g carbohydrates

Peel and dice onions. In a pan, heat 5 tablespoons oil and sauté until golden brown, then remove and drain on paper towels. Clean pan.

Rinse chicken livers under cold running water, pat dry, and remove all blood vessels and membranes. Chop livers finely. Heat another 5 tablespoons oil in the pan, sauté livers, and drain on paper towels.

Place tomatoes in boiling water for 10–15 seconds. Remove from water, peel, cut in half, remove cores and seeds, and dice very finely. Peel eggs and chop.

Thoroughly mix together livers, onions, tomatoes, and eggs and season with salt and pepper. Stir in 5 tablespoons olive oil. Brush bread with remaining oil and toast bread slices until golden brown, before spreading with liver mixture. Chop 1 additional egg and sprinkle over top with parsley.

Crostini with chicken livers are ideally served with large, meaty, green or black olives.

French baguettes are the ideal size for appetizer canapés, but you don't always have to use white bread. You can use darker, heartier types of bread, such as whole-grain and rye, as long as they go well with the topping and you cut them to an appropriate size. Most types of bread do well with a little toasting before being topped. It keeps them crispy longer and brings out a bit more flavor.

Serves 4:
2 large tomatoes
2 tablespoons extra virgin olive oil
Salt (preferably kosher or sea)
Freshly ground black pepper
For the cheese mixture:
$1/2$ red bell pepper
10 ounces feta
2 tablespoons chopped herbs (parsley, thyme, basil)
2 tablespoons olive oil
1 tablespoon Cognac
Plus:
12 slices of a baguette
$1/4$ cup butter
12 basil leaves

Prep time: 30 minutes
(+ 30 minutes refrigeration time)
Per serving approx: 472 calories
13 g protein/38 g fat/19 g carbohydrates

Rinse tomatoes, remove cores, slice, and place in a shallow dish. Combine oil, salt, and pepper, pour over tomato slices, and marinate for 30 minutes.

Rinse bell pepper, remove stem, seeds, and ribs, and dice very finely. Crumble cheese with a fork, salt sparingly (first check salt content of cheese), season with pepper, and sprinkle with herbs. Stir in diced bell peppers, oil, and Cognac and marinate spiced feta for 15 minutes.

Spread baguette slices thinly with butter. Lay 2 slightly overlapping tomato slices on each piece of bread, top with marinated feta, and garnish with basil.

Herbs, feta, and tomatoes arranged on a baguette taste wonderfully fresh — perfect for hot summer days.

Baguette Niçoise

This sharp paste made from olives, anchovies, and capers is not just a good spread for bread but also tastes delicious with cooked pasta.

Serves 6:
12 anchovy fillets
¼ cup capers
1 cup pitted black olives
1 clove garlic
6 tablespoons extra virgin olive oil
1 teaspoon Cognac
Freshly ground black pepper
Plus:
1 baguette
8 pimento stuffed green olives

Prep time: 20 minutes
Per serving approx: 374 calories
9 g protein/23 g fat/34 g carbohydrates

Chop anchovy fillets finely and place in a blender with capers and black olives. Peel garlic, squeeze through a press, and add.

Pour olive oil into blender and process contents to a smooth paste (takes about 2 minutes). Transfer olive mixture to a bowl and season with Cognac and a lot of pepper.

Cut baguette on an angle into 15 slices and spread with tapenade. Cut green olives in half and use to garnish the canapés.

Tapanade takes no time at all to prepare. Sealed in a nice jar, it also makes a wonderful gift from your kitchen. This spicy paste keeps in the refrigerator for at least 2 weeks.

When decorating cold appetizers, there's no limit to what you can do. You can take perfectly simple ingredients like salami and pickles and turn them into works of art in almost no time. The garnish ingredients in the following recipe are only suggestions; feel free to vary them however you wish.

Serves 6:
1¼ pounds salami, some sliced, some in 1-inch cubes
For the garnish:
Quail eggs
Green and black olives
Capers
Cherry tomatoes
Radishes
Yellow and red bell peppers
Pickled vegetables (gherkins, cocktail onions, chili peppers, baby corn)
Plus:
Toothpicks
Fluted paper candy cups (optional)

Place quail eggs in a pot, cover with hot water, and boil for 5 minutes. Remove, rinse under cold water, and peel.

Slice olives or leave whole as desired. Drain capers. Rinse cherry tomatoes and cut in half. Rinse radishes, clean, and slice. Rinse bell peppers, cut in half, remove stems, seeds and ribs, and cut into diamonds. Drain pickled vegetables and, depending on size, cut in half.

Garnish salami with the various ingredients depending on your tastes and fasten together with toothpicks. If you want, you can serve these salami morsels in small fluted paper candy cups. Serve with a fresh baguette.

ese hearty tidbits are also suitable
an outdoor buffet. They're hardy
ough to survive a little sun.

With Crabmeat Filling

Serves 6:
1 sheet phyllo pastry
(15 x 20 inches, 1½ ounces)
Melted butter
For the filling:
12 ounces crabmeat
½ red bell pepper
½ green bell pepper
2–3 scallions
1 small red chili pepper
½ clove garlic
For the sauce:
5 tablespoons mayonnaise
½ teaspoon curry powder
2 tablespoons light soy sauce
1 dash lime juice
Salt (preferably kosher or sea)
Freshly ground black pepper
1 tablespoon chopped herbs
(dill, chives, parsley)
Plus:
1 mini-muffin tin with 12 cups
1 tablespoon chopped chives
Dill sprigs

Prep time: 50 minutes
Per serving approx: 146 calories
14 g protein/5 g fat/11 g carbohydrates

Place 3 phyllo squares in each muffin cup and press pastry down so you will be able to fill it.

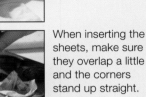

When inserting the sheets, make sure they overlap a little and the corners stand up straight.

Bake pastry in an oven preheated to 350°F for 6–8 minutes until golden brown. Carefully remove from muffin tin.

Carefully spread out phyllo sheet on a work surface and brush on a thin coating of melted butter. Cut pastry into 2½-inch squares. Brush muffin tin with melted butter and continue as described in the photos on the next page.

For the filling, pick over crabmeat well and make sure to check for small pieces of shell. Rinse bell peppers, remove stems, seeds, and ribs, and dice finely. Rinse scallions, clean, and cut into thin rings. Rinse chili pepper, cut in half, remove stem, seeds, and ribs, and chop finely. Peel garlic and chop finely. Combine all prepared ingredients with crabmeat.

For the sauce, thoroughly mix all ingredients and pour over the crabmeat mixture. Fill pre-baked phyllo cups, sprinkle with chives and garnish with dill. Serve immediately.

With Shrimp Filling

Serves 6:
1 sheet phyllo pastry
(15 x 20 inches, 1½ ounces)
Melted butter
For the filling:
12 ounces peeled, cooked
shrimp
½ large red bell pepper
2–3 scallions
1 clove garlic
1 small green chili pepper
For the salad dressing:
3 tablespoons sunflower oil
Salt (preferably kosher or sea)
1 teaspoon lime juice
2 tablespoons light soy sauce
1 teaspoon cilantro
Plus:
1 mini-muffin tin with 12 cups

Prep time: 50 minutes
Per serving approx: 151 calories
13 g protein/8 g fat/
7 g carbohydrates

Spread out pastry sheet on a work surface and brush on a thin coating of melted butter. Cut pastry into 2½-inch squares. Brush muffin tin with melted butter. With dry hands, lay 3 phyllo squares in each muffin cup and gently press pastry down, making sure the entire cup is covered and the ends of the phyllo are pointing straight up. Bake pastry in an oven preheated to 350°F for 6–8 minutes until golden brown and carefully remove phyllo cups from muffin tin.

For the filling, bake bell pepper in an oven preheated to 425°F until the peel blisters. Remove pepper and place in a plastic bag so that it sweats. Then peel, remove stem, seeds, and ribs, and dice finely. Clean scallions and cut into thin rings. Peel garlic and chop finely. Remove stem from chili pepper, cut in half, remove seeds and ribs, and dice finely.

For the dressing, combine sunflower oil, salt, lime juice, and soy sauce. Place diced bell pepper, scallion rings, garlic, chili pepper, chopped cilantro, and shrimp in a bowl. Pour dressing over the top, cover, and marinate in the refrigerator for 30 minutes. Remove and season shrimp to taste with salt and pepper. Wait until just before serving to transfer marinated shrimp to the baked phyllo cups so they won't get soggy.

Tartlets
Filled with Vegetables

Serves 6:

For the short dough:

3 cups flour

6 tablespoons butter

Salt (preferably kosher or sea)

1 small egg yolk

1–2 tablespoons cold water as needed

For the salad:

1 small carrot

1 piece jicama (about the size of a tangerine)

¾ cup sugar snap peas

10–12 thin green beans

½ cup shelled peas

2 tablespoons shallots

½ large red bell pepper

For the dressing:

6 tablespoons mayonnaise

½ teaspoon medium-hot mustard

Salt (preferably kosher or sea)

Freshly ground black pepper

Lemon juice

1 tablespoon herbs (parsley, chives, thyme)

Plus:

20 small molds

Butter

1 canned black truffle cut into strips

Prep time: 1 hour

(+ 30 minutes refrigeration time)

Per serving approx: 419 calories

8 g protein/18 g fat/55 g carbohydrates

Process ingredients listed for the short dough. Wrap in plastic wrap and refrigerate for 30 minutes. Grease molds lightly and place side by side. Then roll out dough thinly, lay over the top of the molds, and roll over it with a rolling pin to score the dough. Gently press dough into the molds and cut off any excess. Pierce the dough bases with a fork and bake the tartlets in an oven preheated to 350°F for 10–12 minutes without opening the oven door.

Peel or clean vegetables. Finely dice carrots and jicama. Cut sugar peas into diamonds. Cut up beans. Boil a small pot of salted water and cook prepared vegetables (except for the jicama) with the peas for 5–8 minutes. Rinse under cold water and drain. Peel shallots, dice finely along with bell pepper, and add along with jicama. Combine all dressing ingredients and mix with vegetables. Transfer vegetable salad to tartlets and garnish with truffle strips.

Serves 4:
$1/2$ sushi rice recipe (see below)
1 bunch chives
2 teaspoons wasabi powder
12 ounces fresh tuna fillet
Plus:
Japanese soy sauce
Pickled ginger

Prep time: 1 hour
Per serving approx: 223 calories
23 g protein/1 g fat/30 g carbohydrates

Prepare rice as described below. Rinse chives, drain briefly, and pat dry. Mix wasabi powder with 3–4 teaspoons water to make a paste and set aside.

Smooth any frayed edges of tuna with a sharp knife. Cut fillet into 8 thin slices, diagonal to the grain, and pat dry with paper towels.

Coat one side of fish pieces with a paper-thin layer of wasabi. Moisten your hands and form sushi rice into oblong balls of 1 tablespoon each. Place one piece of fish in the palm of one hand with the wasabi side facing up. Set a rice ball on top and gently press it onto the fish. Turn sushi over and form it into an even shape. Garnish with chives cut into 1–2-inch pieces and arrange on a platter. Serve with soy sauce, remaining wasabi paste, and pickled ginger.

Sushi Rice

Serves 8:
1 cup sushi rice
2 tablespoons rice vinegar
1 level tablespoon sugar
1 teaspoon salt

Rinse sushi rice in a strainer under cold running water until the water runs clear and drain well.

Bring rice to a boil in $1 1/4$ cups water, boil for 2 minutes and then reduce heat, cover, and cook over low heat for 10 minutes. Remove cover, wedge a double layer of paper towel between the lid and pot (using the lid to hold the paper towel above the rice), and let rice cool for another 10 to 15 minutes.

In the meantime, bring rice vinegar, sugar, and salt to a boil and let cool. Transfer rice to a bowl, drizzle seasoned vinegar over the top and work it in with a wooden fork but don't stir. Cover with a damp cloth until you're ready to use it.

Serve Maguro (tuna sushi) with Japanese soy sauce and Wasabi paste as dips, as well as some sweet and spicy pickled ginger.

Nigiri Sushi with Shrimp

Serves 4:
½ sushi rice recipe (page 62)
8 raw, unpeeled shrimp
Salt (preferably kosher or sea)
2 teaspoons wasabi powder
2 tablespoons rice vinegar
2 teaspoons rice wine (Mirin)
Plus:
Japanese soy sauce
Pickled ginger

Prep time: 1 hour
Per serving approx: 190 calories
15 g protein/1 g fat/30 g carbohydrates

Rinse shrimp and cook in simmering, salted water over low heat for 4-5 minutes. Remove and plunge into ice water. Mix wasabi powder with 3–4 teaspoons water and set aside.

Peel shrimp except for the tail. Remove the dark vein running along the back. Slit open shrimp on the belly side but leave about ½ inch still attached at both ends.

Combine rice vinegar and rice wine, stir in shrimp, and marinate for 2 minutes. Remove, pat slightly dry, and bend the two halves away from one another, forming a ring. Coat the inside with a paper-thin layer of wasabi paste.

Moisten your hands, form 1 tablespoon sushi rice into a ball, and flatten it slightly on top. Place the shrimp on top of this rice pillow and carefully press the shrimp down and together. Serve shrimp sushi with soy sauce, remaining wasabi, and pickled ginger.

Ebi (shrimp sushi) are both an aromatic and colorful appetizer for any party. You can also prepare the rice and fish and let your guests make their own.

All sushi dishes are based on a Japanese round-grain rice mixed with a combination of vinegar, salt, and sugar. In the case of maki sushi, rice surrounds a filling and is in turn wrapped in seaweed leaves using a bamboo mat.

Serves 6:

For 1 quart dashi stock:
1 ounce kombu (seaweed)
$\frac{1}{2}$ cup bonito flakes

For the sushi:
1 cup tofu
2 tablespoons light soy sauce
1 teaspoon lime juice
Salt (preferably kosher or sea)
Freshly ground black pepper
1$\frac{1}{4}$ cups Japanese round-grain rice
$\frac{2}{3}$ cups wild rice, soaked overnight
1$\frac{1}{4}$ cups vegetable stock
4 tablespoons rice vinegar
1$\frac{1}{2}$ teaspoons sugar

Plus:
Spinach leaves
Salt (preferably kosher or sea)
Freshly ground black pepper
1 red chili pepper (without seeds) cut into strips
4 nori sheets (seaweed)
1 bamboo mat
Flying fish roe

Prep time: 2 hours
Per serving approx: 388 calories
15 g protein/6 g fat/68 g carbohydrates

For the dashi stock, place kombu in 1 quart cold water and bring to a boil over low heat in 10–15 minutes. When bubbles start rising, use your fingernail to check whether the seaweed is soft. Remove seaweed and add $\frac{1}{3}$ cup cold water to liquid. Add bonito flakes and bring to a boil again. As soon as the stock boils, remove pot from heat and wait until the fish flakes sink. Then strain stock through a fine sieve or cheesecloth.

Measure out 1 cup of the dashi stock and keep the rest for some other use or freeze. Cut tofu for sushi into sticks with a thickness of about $\frac{1}{2}$ inch. Stir soy sauce and lime juice into stock, season with salt and pepper, and pour into a shallow dish. Marinate tofu sticks in stock.

Rinse glutinous rice several times until the water runs clear and drain well. In a pot that has a tight-sealing lid, bring rice and 1$\frac{1}{2}$ cups water to a boil. Boil for 2 minutes and then reduce heat. Cover and cook rice for 15 minutes. Remove from heat, wedge a double layer of paper towel between the lid and pot, and let rice cool for another 15 minutes. In the meantime, cook pre-soaked wild rice in vegetable stock for about 40 minutes.

Combine vinegar, sugar, and 1$\frac{1}{2}$ teaspoons salt and heat until the sugar has dissolved. Place white rice in a shallow container and work in vinegar mixture with a wooden fork, without stirring the rice. Remove tofu sticks from marinade. Blanch spinach leaves, season, and wrap around tofu sticks. Wave nori sheets back and forth over an open flame until they turn dark-green and develop an intense aroma. Continue as shown in the two photos on the right.

Spread 1 nori sheet on a bamboo mat and distribute cooked, marinated glutinous rice on top, leaving a ½-inch border of paper around the outside that is not covered by rice. Be careful to dip your hands in vinegar water first to keep the rice from sticking.

Top with wild rice and wrapped tofu sticks. Sprinkle with chili strips. Lift end of bamboo mat and use to roll up sushi tightly, starting from the right side of the nori.

Roll up maki sushi using a bamboo mat. Then remove the mat, moisten the edge of the nori sheet, and press together firmly. Cut roll into ½-inch slices and garnish with a little caviar as desired.

Warm Appetizers

Whether it's meatballs right out of the oven or lemon grass shrimp straight off the grill, people love warm starters on tooth-picks or small skewers. Mini-pizzas, samosas, and empanadas on the other hand, make great finger food. Appetizers, while small, can be the highlight of any meal and can showcase your kitchen skills as much as any entrée.

Shrimp on Lemon Grass Skewers

Serves 4:
4 lemon grass stalks
16 raw, peeled shrimp
For the marinade:
2 tablespoons shallots
2 cloves garlic
2–3 medium-hot chili peppers
1/4 cup pickled ginger, sliced
1 tablespoon dark soy sauce
3 tablespoons peanut oil
1/4 teaspoon coarsely chopped coriander seeds
1/4 teaspoon freshly ground white pepper

Prep time: 30 minutes
(+ 1 hour marinating time)
Per serving approx: 143 calories
6 g protein/11 g fat/6 g carbohydrates

For the marinade, peel shallots and garlic and mince. Remove seeds and ribs from chili peppers and dice very finely. Dice ginger very finely. Mix shallots, garlic, chili peppers, ginger, soy sauce, oil, coriander, and pepper to make a marinade.

Cut lemon grass stalks in half lengthwise. Pierce shrimp with a sharp knife and place two on each half-stalk of lemon grass. Place skewers side by side in the marinade for at least 1 hour, turning occasionally.

Remove skewers from marinade and drain. Cook shrimp skewers on a pre-heated grill for about 1 minute on each side.

A clever way to grill. Using lemon grass stalks as skewers adds subtle flavor and aroma to the shrimp both in the marinade and on the grill.

Folding samosas can take a little getting used to if you are a beginner, so consider trying a "dry run" using strips of paper.

Serves 6:

For the dough:
2 cups flour
1 teaspoon salt
(preferably kosher or sea)
2 tablespoons oil
½ cup warm water

For the filling:
9 ounces lean lamb
⅔ cup onions
1 clove garlic
½ red chili pepper
3 tablespoons oil

2 teaspoons freshly grated ginger
½ teaspoon ground coriander
2 teaspoons curry powder
1 tablespoon lemon juice
½ cup lamb or veal stock
1 tablespoon tomato paste
1 tablespoon chopped mint leaves

For the tomato raita:
1½ cups yogurt
2 tablespoons onions
½ tomato, without peel or seeds
Salt (preferably kosher or sea)
Freshly ground black pepper

1 teaspoon chopped cilantro
1 pinch ground cumin
Plus:
1 egg white
Vegetable oil for deep-frying
Cilantro for garnish

Prep time: 1 hour
(+ 2 hours refrigeration time)
Per serving approx: 371 calories
16 g protein/16 g fat/
40 g carbohydrates

For the dough, sift flower, mix with salt, and form a well in the center. Pour in oil and half the water and stir while gradually mixing in flour from around the edges. Knead into a smooth, pliable dough while gradually working in remaining water. Shape dough into a ball, wrap in plastic wrap, and refrigerate for 2 hours.

Cut lamb into ¼-inch cubes. Peel onions and chop finely. Peel garlic and crush. Remove stem, seeds, and ribs from chili pepper and chop finely.

In a pan, heat oil and sauté onions until translucent. Add garlic, chili pepper pieces, ginger, coriander, curry powder, and lemon juice and cook briefly. Add meat and brown while stirring. Pour in stock, cover, and stew over low heat until the liquid disappears. Add tomato paste and sauté briefly, then add mint. Remove from heat and let filling cool.

For the tomato raita, beat yogurt vigorously. Peel onions and chop finely. Chop tomato flesh finely. Stir both ingredients into yogurt along with salt, pepper, and herbs.

Knead dough briefly and roll out on a lightly floured work surface into a thin square about 16 inches on each side. Cut into 2 x 8-inch strips and make samosas as shown in the photo.

In a deep pan or deep-fryer, heat vegetable oil over medium heat and deep-fry filled samosas in batches for 2–3 minutes until golden. Remove and drain on paper towels. Serve with tomato raita and garnish with a little cilantro.

Samosas are made by folding up the strips of dough. First place 1 teaspoon filling at one end of a dough strip and fold the end diagonally over the top. Continue folding dough diagonally until you've come to the end of the strip. Brush egg white on the end and press together firmly so the samosa won't come apart when you deep-fry it.

The outside of these cheese pockets is a yeast dough that expands nicely when deep-fried. To keep the filling from escaping, make sure that the edges are pressed tightly together for both recipes.

Serves 8:
For the dough:
4 cups flour
2 packets dry yeast
(1½ tablespoons)
½ cup lukewarm water
1 tablespoon sugar
3 eggs
1 tablespoon salt
(preferably kosher or sea)
4 tablespoons softened butter
For the mozzarella-ricotta filling:
5 ounces mozzarella, shredded
½ cup ricotta
2 egg yolks
1 tablespoon chopped basil
¼ cup white bread crumbs
Salt (preferably kosher or sea)
Freshly ground black pepper
24 basil leaves

For the bacon-ricotta filling:
4 ounces bacon
¾ cup onions
1 tablespoon olive oil
1 tablespoon chopped parsley
1½ cups ricotta
Salt (preferably kosher or sea)
Freshly ground black pepper
Plus:
1 egg yolk
2 tablespoons water
Vegetable oil for deep-frying

Prep time: 1 hour
(+ 1 hour proofing time)
Per serving approx:
542 calories
19 g protein/28 g fat/
52 g carbohydrates

Place 1 teaspoon mozzarella filling in the center of each of 24 dough circles with 3-inch diameters.

Place 1 small basil leaf on each teaspoon of mozzarella filling and brush edges with egg yolk.

Sift flour. Dissolve yeast in water and add to flour along with sugar, eggs, salt, and butter. Knead into a smooth, elastic dough. Cover and let rise in a warm place for about 30 minutes.

In the meantime, make the mozzarella filling. In a bowl, combine mozzarella with ricotta, egg yolks, basil, and bread crumbs and season with salt and pepper.

For the bacon filling, dice bacon finely. Peel onions and chop finely. Heat oil and sauté onions until translucent. Fry bacon for 3–4 minutes, stir in parsley, and let cool. Add ricotta and season with salt and pepper.

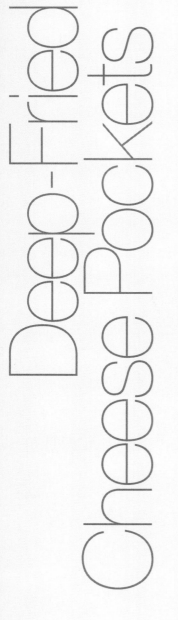

Deep-fry pockets in oil heated to 350°F for 3–4 minutes while stirring.

Divide dough in half. Roll out both dough halves on a floured work surface into sheets ⅛-inch thick. From one sheet, cut out 24 circles with a 3-inch diameter. Top with mozzarella filling as described in the first two steps in the photos on the left. Brush circles with egg yolk and fold shut. Press edges together tightly. Let pockets rise for 10 minutes and then deep-fry as shown in the last photo. From the second sheet, cut out 48 circles with a 2-inch diameter. Place 1 teaspoon of bacon filling on half the circles, place the other circles on top and press edges together tightly. Let rise for 10 minutes. Then deep-fry these pockets too in 350°F oil for 3–4 minutes.

Spring roll wrappers can be filled in a number of ways. Regardless of how they're rolled or folded, the result after deep-frying is always a light, crispy coating. In this recipe, they're rolled into cones that enclose delicious shrimp with a hearty stuffing. The ginger gives this appetizer an Asian touch.

Serves 4:
24 jumbo shrimp (1¼–1½ pounds)
For the filling:
¾ cup bean sprouts
2 cloves garlic
12 ounces pork
6–7 scallions
1 tablespoon oil
1 teaspoon finely chopped ginger
Salt (preferably kosher or sea)
Freshly ground black pepper
2 tablespoons chopped mint
Plus:
12 round spring roll wrappers (8-inch diameter)
1 slightly beaten egg white
Plus:
Vegetable oil for deep-frying

Prep time: 50 minutes
Per serving approx: 496 calories
55 g protein/18 g fat/30 g carbohydrates

Cut wrappers in half and brush edges with egg white. Angle shrimp on the left with the tail at about the center and distribute filling on top.

Starting from the left, roll spring roll wrapper into a cone. Fold in the open edges. Cover with a damp cloth and refrigerate until you're ready to deep-fry them.

Peel shrimp except for the tails and remove vein running along the back. Butterfly 16 of the shrimp by cutting them down the back almost but not completely through. Do this from the head of the shrimp to within ¼ inch of the tail.

For the filling, chop remaining shrimp finely. Blanch bean sprouts in boiling, salted water for 1 minute, drain, and cut into pieces about 1 inch long. Peel garlic and chop finely. Dice pork finely. Clean scallions and slice thinly.

In a pan or wok, heat oil slightly and sauté ginger and garlic until translucent. Add pork and onions and brown. Add chopped shrimp and stir-fry until pink. Season with salt and pepper and let mixture cool. Stir in bean sprouts and chopped mint. Spoon filling between the two sides of the shrimp, created from butterflying. Roll up in wrappers as described in the photos.

To deep-fry the shrimp, heat oil to 350°F in a wok or fryer. Deep-fry shrimp packets in batches for about 3 minutes. Remove with a slotted spoon and drain well on several layers of paper towel.

Serve the crispy fried shrimp immediately because they taste best hot. Provide enough napkins or a bowl of lemon water, or both, so guests can clean their fingers.

Tender seafood shouldn't be exposed to high heat for very long when you cook it, which is what makes it so good for quick deep-frying in a spring roll wrapper.

Serves 4:

For the shrimp-mushroom filling:	For the chili sauce:
2 cloves garlic	1 clove garlic
⅓ cup red onion	2 scallions
1 teaspoon fresh galangal root	1 red chili pepper cut into rings
2 red chili peppers	10 tablespoons light soy sauce
6–8 shiitake or oyster mushrooms	**Plus:**
1 piece lemon grass	8 chives
(about 1 inch long)	8 spring roll wrappers
½ cup fresh bean sprouts	(8–9-inch squares)
10 ounces raw peeled shrimp	1 egg white
5 tablespoons peanut oil	Vegetable oil for deep-frying
3 tablespoons light soy sauce	
2 tablespoons fish sauce	Prep time: 40 minutes
Salt (preferably kosher or sea)	Per serving approx: 434 calories
Freshly ground black pepper	26 g protein/19 g fat/
5 finely chopped Thai basil leaves	40 g carbohydrates

Peel garlic, onion, and galangal. Chop garlic and galangal finely. Finely slice onions. Cut chili peppers in half, remove stems, seeds, and ribs, and dice finely. Clean mushrooms, remove stems if using shitakes, and slice caps thinly. Chop lemon grass finely. Sort bean sprouts. Rinse shrimp, drain well, and dice finely.

In a wok, heat 2 tablespoons oil and briefly stir-fry galangal, garlic, chili peppers, onion slices, and lemon grass. Add bean sprouts and mushrooms and sauté for 1 minute. Remove and set aside.

Heat remaining oil in wok and stir-fry shrimp for 2 minutes. Add vegetables again and mix together. Stir in soy and fish sauce and season with salt and pepper if desired. Add basil and let cool.

Blanch chives in boiling salted water for 5 seconds and drain. Lay wrappers out on a work surface and put a little filling in the middle of each. Brush edges with egg white and wrap up filling in small packets. Make sure the filling can't escape. Bind each packet with 1 chive.

For the sauce, peel garlic and chop finely. Clean scallions and cut into thin rings. Stir chili rings, scallion rings, and garlic into soy sauce.

In a deep-fryer, heat oil to 350°F, and deep-fry shrimp rolls. Remove, drain, and serve. Serve sauce on the side.

Serves 6:
15 sheets frozen puff pastry
(4 x 4 inches)
For the filling:
1 ounce smoked bacon
1/3 cup peeled onions
1 piece celery root
(about the size of a walnut)
1/4 carrot, cleaned
1 green chili pepper
1/2 clove garlic
1 tablespoon tomato paste
2 tablespoons dry sherry
1/2 cup beef stock
Salt (preferably kosher or sea)
2 teaspoons Hungarian
sweet paprika

7 ounces chopped meat
(mixture of beef and pork)
1 egg yolk
1 tablespoon chopped parsley
Plus:
Flour for the work surface
1 egg yolk
2 tablespoons milk
Parchment paper for the baking sheet
Black sesame seeds
Coarse salt

Prep time: 40 minutes
(+ 20 minutes refrigeration time)
Per serving approx: 814 calories
17 g protein/57 g fat/
57 g carbohydrates

Let puff pastry thaw on a lightly floured work surface.

For the filling, dice bacon finely. Cut onions, celery root, and carrots into small cubes. Rinse chili pepper, remove stem, seeds, and ribs, and dice finely. Peel garlic and crush. Fry bacon until translucent. Add and brown diced onion, celery root, carrots, and garlic. Stir in tomato paste and sherry and sauté over high heat for 2 minutes. Pour in stock. Stir in diced chili pepper and reduce over moderate heat until the mixture is relatively dry. Transfer to a bowl and let cool slightly.

Work ground meat, egg yolk, and parsley into the bacon-vegetable mixture and season to taste with salt and paprika.

Whisk egg yolk with milk. Cut puff pastry squares in half crosswise and brush edges with whisked egg yolk. Place 1 teaspoon filling in the middle of each and carefully fold pastry into pockets, pressing edges together tightly with a fork. Place pockets on a baking sheet lined with parchment paper and refrigerate for 20 minutes.

Brush pockets with remaining whisked egg yolk. Sprinkle with sesame seeds and coarse salt and bake in an oven preheated to 400°F until they appear golden brown.

Instead of black sesame seeds, you can also sprinkle meat pockets with light sesame seeds, caraway seeds, or poppy seeds. But be sure to use coarse salt in any case.

Shrimp Empanadas

The cornmeal used for this recipe is made from shelled white corn kernels that have first been soaked in warm water containing lime and can be found in Mexican specialty shops. Jalapeño peppers provide spiciness to the filling and sauce. If you don't like it so hot, remove the seeds and ribs before working with the peppers further.

Serves 6:
2 cups masa harina
(Mexican cornmeal)
½ teaspoon salt
(preferably kosher or sea)
1 teaspoon Hungarian
sweet paprika
4 tablespoons vegetable oil
1¼–1½ cups water
For the filling:
12 ounces peeled, cooked shrimp
¼ cup white onions
4 cloves garlic
1 tomato
1 jalapeño pepper
4 tablespoons oil
1 teaspoon ground allspice

1 teaspoon dried oregano
Salt (preferably kosher or sea)
For the Mexican salsa:
3 medium tomatoes
¾ cup chopped onion
2 jalapeño peppers
2 tablespoons chopped cilantro
2 teaspoons lime juice
Salt (preferably kosher or sea)
Plus:
Oil for deep-frying

Prep time: 1¼ hours
(+ 1 hour proofing time)
Per serving approx: 476 calories
19 g protein/22 g fat/
52 g carbohydrates

Season cornmeal with salt and paprika. Gradually work in oil and enough water to form a smooth dough. Set aside for 1 hour.

Chop shrimp finely. Peel onions and garlic. Chop onions finely and squeeze garlic through a press. Blanch tomatoes in boiling water for 15–20 seconds, remove peels, cores, and seeds, and dice very finely. Save blanching water. Finely chop jalapeño. Heat oil and sauté onions and garlic until translucent. Add shrimp, tomatoes, diced jalapeno, and spices. Braise until all the liquid is gone.

For the salsa, blanch tomatoes in the same water as before, remove peels, cut in half, remove seeds, and dice coarsely. Remove stems from jalapenos and chop finely. Combine tomatoes, onion, and peppers with cilantro, salt, and lime juice.

Knead dough briefly and divide into 12 pieces. Roll out each piece between two pieces of plastic wrap and cut out 4-inch circles. Roll out the dough scraps as well. Place 1 table-spoon filling on one-half of the dough, fold over the other half, and press together tightly. Notch edges with the back of a knife blade.

In a pan or deep-fryer, heat a large amount of oil to 350°F and deep-fry empanadas for 3–5 minutes until golden brown. Remove and drain well. Serve empanadas immediately with the salsa on the side.

Empanadas should be served hot in both senses of the word — spicy and warm. They're excellent with any variety of Mexican beer.

Mini Pizzas

Serves 6:

For the dough:
2½ cups flour
3 packets dry yeast
(2 heaping tablespoons)
½ cup lukewarm water
2 tablespoons olive oil
½ teaspoon salt
(preferably kosher or sea)

For the tomato sauce:
4 small tomatoes
¾ cup onions
1 clove garlic
4 tablespoons olive oil
2 tablespoons tomato paste
½ teaspoon salt
(preferably kosher or sea)
Freshly ground white pepper

For the topping:
2 yellow bell peppers
1 small white onion
16–20 pitted black olives
2 green chili peppers
9 ounces thinly sliced Italian salami
2 tablespoons chopped herbs
(parsley, basil, thyme, oregano, rosemary)
4 ounces freshly grated Gruyère

Plus:
Oil for the baking sheet
Flour for the work surface

Prep time: 1¼ hours
(+ 30 minutes proofing time)
Per serving approx: 629 calories
24 g protein/36 g fat/52 g carbohydrates

For the dough, sift flour into a bowl and make a well in the center. Crumble yeast into the well and dissolve in water while mixing in a little flour from around the edges until a dough is formed. Dust dough lightly with flour, cover bowl with a dishtowel, and let dough rise in a warm place until cracks form on the surface. Add oil and salt and knead into a smooth dough. Shape into a ball, cover, and let rise until it has doubled in volume.

In the meantime, make the sauce: blanch tomatoes for 15 seconds in boiling water, remove peels, cut into quarters, remove seeds, and dice finely. Peel onions and garlic and chop finely. Heat oil and sauté onions and garlic until translucent. Stir in tomato paste, add tomatoes, and reduce sauce slightly over medium heat. Season with salt and pepper.

For the topping, remove stems, seeds, and ribs from bell peppers and dice. Peel onion, cut in half lengthwise, and slice thinly. Cut olives in half. Remove stems from chili peppers and cut into rings while removing seeds.

Coat two baking sheets with a little oil. Knead dough thoroughly and roll out on a floured work surface into a sheet about ¼-inch thick, then cut out circles with 3-inch diameters. Place dough circles on the baking sheets, pierce several times with a fork and let rise for 10 minutes.

Distribute sauce on dough rounds and top with bell peppers, onions, salami, olives, and chili peppers. Sprinkle with herbs and cheese. Bake pizzas in an oven preheated to 400°F for 15 minutes.

Generously topped and spiced, bite after bite these colorful pizzas are a real treat. Naturally, you can vary the topping—for example, with cooked ham or marinated, cooked chicken.

Cheese Spirals

This recipe will teach you how to throw together a delicious puff pastry dish with very little effort. As far as the cheese is concerned, you're free to use types other than Gouda, which is recommended.

Serves 8:
4 square sheets of frozen puff pastry (8 x 8 inches)
3 ounces freshly grated Gouda
2 tablespoons chopped chives
Freshly ground black pepper
Hungarian sweet paprika
Plus:
1 egg yolk
1 tablespoon water
Flour for the work surface

Prep time: 30 minutes
(+ 30 minutes proofing time)
Per serving approx: 168 calories
5 g protein/12 g fat/10 g carbohydrates

Let puff pastry sheets thaw. On a lightly floured surface, lay out in 8-inch squares.

Whisk egg yolk with water and brush onto pastry squares. Sprinkle ¾ ounce cheese and a quarter of the chives on each square, leaving a ¼-inch margin free at the top and bottom. Season with pepper and paprika.

Roll up pastry sheets. Cut each roll into 16 slices and place on a baking sheet lined with parchment paper. Cover and refrigerate for 30 minutes.

Bake filled pastry rolls in an oven preheated to 400°F for 10–12 minutes until light brown.

These tender little cheese spirals taste best baked until golden and served fresh from the oven.

Three Cheese Rolls

You can serve various dips with these rolls, which have a delicious, melted filling. They're great with a spicy, cold tomato chili sauce or an avocado puree.

Serves 6:
24 spring roll wrappers (5 x 5 inches)
For the filling:
8–10 white mushrooms
1 tablespoon olive oil
6–7 scallions
1 clove garlic
3½ ounces prosciutto
3 eggs
⅔ cup ricotta
6 ounces Gruyère
3½ ounces Parmesan
1 cup finely diced tomato flesh
Finely chopped thyme and rosemary
Salt (preferably kosher or sea)
Freshly ground black pepper
Plus:
1 egg white
Vegetable oil for deep-frying

Prep time: 40 minutes
Per serving approx: 381 calories
25 g protein/22 g fat/22 g carbohydrates

For the filling, clean mushrooms and dice finely. Heat oil and sauté mushrooms without browning. Clean scallions and cut into thin rings. Peel garlic and chop finely. Cut prosciutto into very small cubes. Whisk eggs. Mash ricotta slightly with a fork and finely dice Gruyère and Parmesan.

Combine three types of cheese in a bowl and stir in eggs. Add all prepared ingredients plus diced tomato. Add herbs and season with salt and pepper.

Lay out wrappers on a work surface. Place a little filling in the center of each one. Fold the bottom edge of the wrapper until you have covered the filling, then fold in the two sides and roll it up towards the top of the wrapper. Brush the end of each roll with egg white and press together. In a deep-fryer, heat oil to 350°F and deep-fry rolls until golden brown.

These crispy, deep-fried rolls are packed with three cheeses, prosciutto, and aromatic herbs.

Soy sauce can serve as a simple dip for these crispy wontons. They also taste excellent with the sweet and sour flavor profile of the sauce recommended in the recipe.

Serves 6:
20 spring roll wrappers
(5 x 5 inches)
For the filling:
20 dried shiitake mushrooms
9 ounces boneless,
skinless chicken breasts
¾ cup canned bamboo shoots
¼ cup shelled peas
¼ cup fresh ginger
4 scallions
For the marinade:
1 tablespoon soy sauce
1 tablespoon rice wine
½ teaspoon salt
(preferably kosher or sea)
Freshly ground white pepper
1 teaspoon sesame oil

1 teaspoon cornstarch
For the sweet and sour sauce:
1 pound red bell peppers
2 cloves garlic
Flesh from 5 small red
chili peppers
½ cup mild rice vinegar
2 cups sugar
½ teaspoon salt
Plus:
Peanut oil for deep-frying

Prep time: 2 hours
Per serving approx:
493 calories
16 g protein/2 g fat/
103 g carbohydrates

Pour marinade over meat and prepared vegetables, marinate 5–10 minutes, and remove.

Place filling on the wrappers. First fold the bottom until the filling is completely covered by the wrapper. Fold the top down so it rests on top of the filling and then fold the sides in and secure with a few drops of warm water.

First prepare the sauce. Remove stems, seeds, and ribs from bell peppers, and chop coarsely. Peel garlic. Cut chili flesh into strips.

Crush bell peppers, garlic, and chilies in a mortar to make a paste. Transfer paste to a pot and pour in 1 cup water. Stir in vinegar, sugar, and salt and bring to a boil. Lower heat and reduce mixture for about 30 minutes to make a thick sauce.

For the filling, soak dried shiitake mushrooms in hot water for 20 minutes. Remove from water and squeeze out thoroughly. Remove hard stems and cut caps into thin strips.

Rinse chicken briefly under cold running water, pat dry, and cut on an angle into thin, uniform strips. If necessary, cut strips in half crosswise.

Drain bamboo shoots well and cut into strips. Cook peas in boiling, salted water. Peel ginger and chop finely. Clean scallions and cut into thin rings.

For the marinade, combine all the ingredients listed in a small bowl and use to marinate all prepared ingredients as described in the first photo to the right.

Heat oil and deep-fry wontons for about 4 minutes, stirring occasionally with a wire ladle or slotted spoon.

Spread out spring roll wrappers on a work surface and make the wontons as described in the center photo. In a wok or deep-fryer, heat oil to 350°F and fry wontons until golden as described in the last photo in the series.

Remove wontons, drain briefly on paper towels, and serve immediately with sweet and sour sauce.

Golden-Fried Cod

Serves 4:
14 ounces cod, cleaned
Salt (preferably kosher or sea)
Freshly ground black pepper
For the tartar sauce:
1 egg
1/2 teaspoon wine vinegar
1/4 teaspoon hot mustard
1/2 teaspoon salt
(preferably kosher or sea)
1/4 teaspoon white pepper
3/4 cup sunflower oil
1 hard-boiled egg, peeled
1/2 cup pickles
3 anchovy fillets
1 tablespoon capers
1 tablespoon chopped tarragon

1 tablespoon chopped chervil
1 teaspoon chopped chives
1 teaspoon chopped parsley
Cayenne pepper
Plus:
2 eggs
Flour
3/4 cup bread crumbs
4 tablespoons oil
2 tablespoons butter
1 medium cucumber cut into 1/8-inch slices
Dill sprigs
Lemon wedges

Prep time: 30 minutes
Per serving approx: 853 calories
24 g protein/50 g fat/20 g carbohydrates

Cut cod into pieces about 3 inches long, cut these pieces in half lengthwise, and season with salt and pepper.

For the sauce, mix egg, vinegar, mustard, salt, and pepper in a blender at the lowest speed until smooth while drizzling in a thin stream of oil. Transfer sauce to a bowl. Finely dice hard-boiled egg, pickles, anchovy fillets, and capers. Stir into sauce along with herbs and add seasoning.

Whisk eggs. Dredge cod pieces in flour, then egg, and then bread crumbs. Heat oil and butter and sauté cod until golden brown and crispy. Remove, drain, and garnish with cucumber slices, dill, and a few lemon wedges. Serve sauce on the side.

Tartar sauce doesn't just go with fried cod. You can also serve it with any dish that calls for a fresh, cool sauce.

Involtini di Vitello

Serves 6:

10 ounces trimmed veal fillets	1 teaspoon chopped thyme
Salt (preferably kosher or sea)	1 pinch lemon zest
Freshly ground black pepper	2 tablespoons olive oil
4 ounces raw, smoked ham	1 tablespoon lemon juice
20 medium-sized sage leaves	Salt (preferably kosher or sea)
2 tablespoons olive oil	Freshly ground black pepper
40 kalamata olives	**Plus:**
20 thin slices of lemon	20 wooden skewers
For the marinade:	
1 clove garlic	Prep time: 1 hour
1 tablespoon chopped parsley	Per serving approx: 139 calories
1 teaspoon chopped rosemary	15 g protein/7 g fat/3 g carbohydrates

Cut veal fillets into slices of about ½-inch thick (you should get 20 slices). Lay each individual slice between sheets of plastic wrap and pound flat. Season with salt and pepper.

Cut ham into 1-inch squares. Place a piece of ham and one sage leaf on top of each meat slice. Fold in the long sides of the veal slices and, starting from one of the narrower ends, roll into roulades.

For the marinade, peel garlic, chop finely, and place in a bowl. Add herbs and lemon zest. Pour in oil and lemon juice and mix thoroughly. Season with salt and pepper.

In a pan, heat oil and brown meat rolls, first with the seam side down and then on all sides. Drizzle with half the marinade, cook another 1–2 minutes, and remove from the pan.

Thread one olive, one meat roll, a folded lemon slice, and another olive onto each skewer. Place skewers in the pan, pour in remaining marinade, and heat briefly.

Garlic, lemon, rosemary, and thyme in the marinade give these tender veal rolls a Mediterranean accent.

Tuscan Pork Skewers

Serves 6:
1 clove garlic
2 teaspoons fresh ginger
1 red chili pepper
6–7 scallions
14 ounces ground pork
Zest from $\frac{1}{2}$ lime
1 egg
Salt (preferably kosher or sea)
Freshly ground black pepper

For the hot bell pepper sauce:
2 large red bell peppers
4 red chili peppers
2 cloves garlic
$\frac{1}{2}$ cup white wine vinegar
2 cups sugar
$\frac{1}{2}$ teaspoon salt
(preferably kosher or sea)

For the vegetables:
2 small zucchini
12 cherry tomatoes
2 tablespoons vegetable oil
Salt (preferably kosher or sea)
Freshly ground black pepper
Plus:
2 tablespoons vegetable oil
24 toothpicks
1 tablespoon chopped parsley

Prep time: 1$\frac{1}{4}$ hours
Per serving approx: 566 calories
15 g protein/20 g fat/
81 g carbohydrates

For the sauce, remove stems, seeds, and ribs from bell peppers and chili peppers, and chop flesh finely. Peel garlic and chop. Finely grind all these ingredients in a mortar. Bring this paste to a boil in 1 cup water, vinegar, sugar, and salt, and simmer over low heat for about 30 minutes.

In the meantime, make the patties. Peel garlic and chop ginger and garlic very finely. Cut chili pepper in half, remove stems, seeds, and ribs, and dice finely. Clean scallions and chop finely. Mix ground meat with ginger, garlic, chili peppers, scallions, lime zest, and egg. Season with salt and pepper. Form the meat mixture into 24 meatballs and press each one slightly flat. Heat oil and fry meat patties on both sides.

Rinse zucchini, clean, and cut into ¼-inch slices. Cut tomatoes in half crosswise and remove cores. Heat oil and sauté zucchini slices briefly on both sides. Add tomatoes and sauté briefly. Season with salt and pepper.

Pierce 1 zucchini slice, 1 patty, and one tomato half with each toothpick. Sprinkle with parsley and serve with the sauce.

Pork Patties au Gratin

Serves 4:
1 clove garlic
1 red chili pepper
6 scallions
14 ounces ground pork
2 teaspoons fresh ginger
Zest from ½ lime
1 egg
Salt (preferably kosher or sea)
Freshly ground black pepper
Plus:
2 tablespoons vegetable oil
½ red onion
4 ounces mozzarella
2 tablespoons chopped chives
12 wooden skewers about 6 inches long

Prep time: 40 minutes
Per serving approx: 444 calories
25 g protein/35 g fat/7 g carbohydrates

Peel and dice garlic very finely. Clean chili pepper, remove seeds and ribs, and chop finely. Chop scallions into thin rings. Mix pork with garlic, pepper, scallions, ginger, and lime zest. Stir in egg and season with salt and pepper. Form into patties and fry in vegetable oil on both sides. Peel onions, cut in half lengthwise, and cut into thin wedges. Add to pan and sauté briefly. Thread two patties and onion wedges onto each skewer and place skewers on a baking sheet.

Cut mozzarella into thin slices 1 x 2 inches and lay on top of the skewers. Broil briefly in an oven preheated to 400°F. Remove, arrange on a platter, sprinkle with chopped chives, and serve. Also goes well with a hot bell pepper sauce as described in the recipe on page 96.

Ginger, garlic, and lime zest lend these spicy meatballs a distinctive flavor.

Seafood Skewers

Serves 4:
1 clove garlic
2 tablespoons olive oil
8 ounces cleaned squid
$\frac{1}{4}$ cup white wine
$\frac{3}{4}$ cup white bread crumbs
1 teaspoon chopped oregano
Juice from $\frac{1}{2}$ lemon
Salt (preferably kosher or sea)
Freshly ground black pepper
8 large raw, peeled shrimp
4 young leeks or 8 scallion whites
8 cherry tomatoes
Plus:
8 wooden skewers

Prep time: 40 minutes
Per serving approx: 240 calories
16 g protein/9 g fat/23 g carbohydrates

Alternately thread leek, squid, tomato, leek, shrimp, and another tomato onto each skewer.

Dredge skewers in remaining bread crumb mixture.

Peel garlic and dice finely. In a pan, heat half the oil and brown garlic and squid. Pour in white wine. Remove squid, set aside, and pour liquid into a shallow bowl.

Add bread crumbs, oregano, lemon juice, salt, and pepper to the liquid and mix thoroughly. Marinate shrimp in this spice mixture.

Clean leeks, rinse, and cut on a slight angle into pieces 1–1½ inches long. Blanch leek pieces in boiling, salted water for 30 seconds. Then remove and plunge into ice water so they'll retain their color and crispness. (If using scallion whites, you do not need to blanch them.)

Rinse tomatoes and remove cores. Thread leek, squid, cherry tomatoes, and marinated shrimp onto wooden skewers as described in the photos and coat with remaining bread mixture.

Drizzle skewers with remaining oil and cook on a preheated grill for 4–5 minutes, turning occasionally. Serve seafood skewers immediately.

Easy to bite into: With a light bread crumb coating and cooked briefly on a hot grill, these skewers give you a taste of Southern Europe by the sea.

Prosciutto-Wrapped Polenta

These morsels are not only good as an appetizer or snack, but also on a warm buffet. Make sure they don't sit around too long or are allowed to cool after you make them because then the polenta will form a hard crust.

Serves 6:
2½ cups vegetable stock
3 tablespoons butter
½ teaspoon salt
(preferably kosher or sea)
3 cups corn grits or instant
polenta (medium grain)
For the tomato sauce:
5 medium tomatoes, ripe
½ small onion, chopped
1 clove garlic
1 small pepperoncino
5 tablespoons olive oil
1 tablespoon chopped parsley

1 tablespoon chopped herbs
Salt (preferably kosher or sea)
Freshly ground black pepper
Plus:
9 ounces thinly sliced prosciutto
About 20 anchovy fillets
2 tablespoons vegetable oil
3 tablespoons butter
Toothpicks

Prep time: 50 minutes
(+ 30 minutes cooling time)
Per serving approx: 616 calories
19 g protein/36 g fat/55 g carbohydrates

Bring stock to a boil with butter and salt. Add corn grits in a thin stream while stirring constantly, making sure the liquid never stops bubbling. Continue stirring clockwise every 2–3 minutes until the porridge comes away from the sides of the pot (about 20 minutes).

Spread polenta on a cutting board or cookie sheet lined with plastic wrap. Let polenta cool and cut into squares measuring 1–1½ inches.

For the sauce, blanch tomatoes in boiling water for 15 seconds, peel, cut in half, remove cores and seeds (rub seeds through a strainer and keep the juice), and dice flesh finely. Peel garlic and chop finely. Remove seeds from pepperoncino and chop finely. Heat oil and sauté onions and garlic until translucent. Add pepperoncino, diced tomato, parsley, and remaining herbs (oregano, sage, rosemary). Pour in tomato juice, cover, and stew over low heat for 15 minutes. Season with salt and pepper.

Cut prosciutto slices into strips 1-inch wide. Rinse anchovy fillets and cut in half crosswise. Continue as described in the photo. Then heat oil and butter and sauté polenta cubes over medium heat for 2–3 minutes. Pierce with a toothpick and serve with tomato sauce.

Lay out the prosciutto strip. Place a polenta cube and half an anchovy fillet on each strip and wrap in the prosciutto.

Italian finger food. These little polenta snacks are wrapped in prosciutto strips, sautéed briefly, and served on toothpicks, perfect for dipping them in the tomato sauce.

Cheese Cubes with Red Currant Sauce

In addition to Camembert, this cheese appetizer can be made with other types of cheese, as long as they have a high fat content.

Serves 4:
For the sauce:
1 red onion
1 cup dried red currants
½ cup currant juice
½ cup sugar
1 whole clove
½ cinnamon stick
For the cheese cubes:
10 ounces Camembert
1 egg
½ cup bread crumbs
⅓ cup finely ground hazelnuts or almonds
Cayenne pepper
Plus:
Vegetable oil for deep-frying

Prep time: 30 minutes
(+ 1 hour soaking time)
Per serving approx: 517 calories
20 g protein/29 g fat/44 g carbohydrates

For the sauce, peel onion and mince.

In a pot, combine onion, currants, currant juice, sugar, clove, and cinnamon stick and let stand for 1 hour. Then bring mixture to a boil and simmer over low heat for 5 minutes until the sauce becomes thick and syrupy. Remove clove and cinnamon stick. Transfer current sauce to a small bowl and let cool.

Cut Camembert into cubes of about ½ inch. Beat egg in a shallow bowl. Mix bread crumbs, nuts, and cayenne in a second bowl.

In a wok or deep-fryer, heat oil. Dredge cheese cubes in egg, roll in bread crumb-nut mixture, and deep-fry in hot oil in batches for 2 minutes. Remove and drain on paper towels. Serve cheese cubes hot, accompanied by the currant sauce.

Skewered Chicken Meatballs

In Japan, these skewers are known as yakitori. They can either be fried in a pan or grilled.

Serves 6:
1 pound boneless, skinless chicken meat
1 teaspoon ginger
2 scallions
½ red bell pepper, cleaned
1 tablespoon chopped parsley
1 egg
1½ tablespoons heavy cream
Salt (preferably kosher or sea)
¼ teaspoon szechuan pepper
5 tablespoons vegetable oil
For the sauce:
1 piece lemon grass (2 inches long)
½ chili pepper cut in half crosswise
1 tablespoon cilantro
¼ cup dark soy sauce
¼ cup mirin
¼ cup sake
2 teaspoons tamari
1 teaspoon brown sugar
Plus:
6–8 bok choy leaves
Wooden skewers

Prep time: 45 minutes
Per serving approx: 321 calories
22 g protein/3 g fat/5 g carbohydrates

Process meat with a meat grinder using the fine cutting disk. Peel ginger and chop finely. Rinse scallions, clean, and dice only the white parts finely. Dice bell pepper finely.

Thoroughly mix together meat, ginger, scallions, bell peppers, and parsley. Work in the egg and stir in cream. Season with salt and szechuan pepper. Moisten your hands and shape the mixture into meatballs of 1 inch in diameter. Clean bok choy, rinse, remove leaves from stems, and cut stems into cubes of about 1 inch. (The leaves are not needed for this recipe.)

For the sauce, clean lemon grass and cut into fine rings. Remove seeds from chili pepper and cut into thin strips. Chop cilantro coarsely. Combine dark soy sauce, mirin, sake, tamari, sugar, lemon grass, chili rings, and cilantro and briefly bring to a boil. Set aside.

Alternately thread meatballs and bok choy onto skewers. In a pan, heat oil and sauté skewers on all sides for 5–6 minutes. Remove and place on pre-warmed plates. Serve sauce on the side.

Chicken and vegetables—these spicy meatballs on a skewer are separated by pieces of bok choy.

Serves 8:

For the meat mixture:
1/2 medium onion
1/2 clove garlic
2 boneless, skinless chicken breasts
7 ounces pork shoulder
1 teaspoon salt (preferably kosher or sea)
Freshly ground black pepper
1 teaspoon Hungarian sweet paprika
1 tablespoon chopped parsley
1 egg
4 slices white bread without the crust

2 tablespoons butter
1/2 cup heavy cream

For the marinade:
1 tablespoon balsamic vinegar
2 tablespoons white wine vinegar
1 dash lemon juice
Salt (preferably kosher or sea)
Freshly ground black pepper
6 tablespoons olive oil
2 tablespoons shallots
1 clove garlic
2 tablespoons chopped herbs (parsley, thyme, rosemary, basil)

Plus:
1 large red bell pepper
1 piece cucumber (about 2 inches)
10 pearl onions
2 tablespoons vegetable oil
3 tablespoons butter
Salt (preferably kosher or sea)
Freshly ground black pepper
20 wooden skewers, 5–6 inches long

Prep time: 55 minutes
Per serving approx: 392 calories
19 g protein/30 g fat/
12 g carbohydrates

For the meat mixture, chop half the onions and garlic. Cut up chicken and pork and process along with onions and garlic with a meat grinder using the medium cutting disk. Season with salt, pepper, and paprika. Stir in parsley and egg.

Cut white bread and remaining onions into small cubes. In a pan, melt butter and sauté onion and bread cubes without browning. Add cream, briefly bring to a rolling boil, and fold onion mixture into meat mixture.

Cut bell pepper in half, remove stem, seeds, and ribs and cut into 20 squares of about 3/4 inch. Peel cucumber, cut in half lengthwise, scrape out seeds with a spoon, and cut slices 1/4-inch thick. Peel pearl onions.

From the meat mixture, make 40 meatballs 1 inch in diameter and press slightly flat. In a pan, heat oil and butter, and fry the meat croquettes for about 2 minutes on each side. Remove from pan, place peppers, cucumbers, and onions in the same pan, and sauté briefly. Season with salt and pepper.

Thread one meatball, one piece of bell pepper, another meatball, and a piece of cucumber or an onion onto a skewer. Arrange skewers on a platter.

For the marinade, mix two types of vinegar, lemon juice, salt, and pepper. Then add oil in a thin stream while stirring constantly. Peel shallots and garlic, chop finely, and add to marinade along with the herbs. Drizzle skewers with marinade and serve.

Cucumbers, onions, and bell pepper balance the meatballs in this recipe, but you can easily vary the vegetable. Zucchini, mushrooms, or cherry tomatoes also go nicely.

In Greece, these meatballs are served with Tzatziki, a refreshing yogurt sauce with cucumber, dill, and a lot of garlic.

Serves 8:
2 slices white bread without the crust
½ medium onion
14 ounces ground beef
14 ounces ground pork
2 tablespoons chopped parsley
1 teaspoon chopped mint
1 tablespoon lemon juice
2 eggs
1 tablespoon olive oil
Salt (preferably kosher or sea)
Freshly ground white pepper
Plus:
Flour for dredging
3–4 tablespoons vegetable oil for frying

Prep time: 30 minutes
(+ 30 minutes refrigeration time)
Per serving approx: 301 calories
20 g protein/22 g fat/5 g carbohydrates

Soak white bread in a little water. Peel onion and chop finely. Squeeze out bread and tear into pieces.

In a bowl, mix ground meat, bread, chopped onions, parsley, mint, lemon juice, eggs, and olive oil. Season with salt and pepper. Refrigerate meat mixture for 30 minutes. Then moisten your hands, shape meat mixture into oblong balls about 1½ inches long, and dredge meatballs in a little flour.

In a pan, heat vegetable oil and brown meatballs on all sides in batches (takes 4–5 minutes). Remove and drain on paper towels.

You can also prepare Keftédes on the grill. In this case, brush oil onto the rack or pan so the meatballs turn easily.

Asian Pork Hedgehogs

While the meatballs steam in a bamboo steamer, be sure to check the water level in the wok now and then and add more if necessary. Instead of a wok, you can just as easily prepare these hedgehogs in a steamer pot made of metal.

Serves 6:
½ cup sushi rice
1¼ pounds pork shoulder
1 small red onion
1 clove garlic
1 tablespoon vegetable oil
1 teaspoon palm sugar
1 tablespoon chopped cilantro
3 tablespoons light soy sauce
1 egg white
1 tablespoon rice wine
Salt (preferably kosher or sea)
Freshly ground black pepper
For the red chili sauce:
2 medium-hot red chili peppers
¼ medium onion

½ clove garlic
1 teaspoon vegetable oil
4 tomatoes, strained
½ teaspoon salt
(preferably kosher or sea)
½ teaspoon sugar
Plus:
Vegetable oil for greasing
bamboo basket

Prep time: 1¼ hours
Per serving approx: 411 calories
23 g protein/24 g fat/
26 g carbohydrates

Moisten your hands and shape prepared meat mixture into 28 balls.

Spread rice on a platter and roll balls around in it until they're evenly coated on all sides.

Rinse rice in a strainer under cold running water and then soak overnight in cold water. Drain well. The next day, chop meat very finely or process with a meat grinder using the finest cutting disk. Refrigerate until ready to use.

Peel onion and garlic and chop finely. In a pan, heat oil, add onion and garlic, sprinkle with sugar, and sauté until translucent. Remove and let cool slightly, then mix with ground meat. Knead in cilantro, soy sauce, egg white, rice wine, salt, and pepper and continue as described in the photos.

Fill a wok ⅓ full with water. Bring water to a boil, place the filled bamboo basket inside, and reduce heat. Cook meatballs for 20–25 minutes.

Brush oil on the bottom of a bamboo steamer and fill with "hedgehogs." Place cover on steamer.

In the meantime, make the sauce: Remove stems, seeds, and ribs from chili peppers and dice finely. Peel onion and garlic and chop both finely. In a pot, heat oil and sauté onions, garlic, and diced chiles without browning. Add strained tomatoes, season with salt and sugar, and simmer sauce for 10 minutes while stirring. Serve sauce on the side with the pork hedgehogs.

These "hedgehogs" are a very distinctive variation on the little Chinese appetizers known as "dim sum," which are usually enjoyed in the morning or early afternoon as a small snack.

Falafel

Serves 6:
3 cups garbanzo beans, canned
$\frac{1}{2}$ medium onion
2 cloves garlic
$\frac{1}{2}$ teaspoon ground cumin
$\frac{1}{2}$ teaspoon ground coriander
$\frac{1}{4}$ teaspoon chili powder
Salt (preferably kosher or sea)
Freshly ground black pepper
1 teaspoon lemon juice
2 tablespoons chopped parsley
1 egg
Plus:
Vegetable oil for deep-frying

Prep time: 30 minutes
Per serving approx: 162 calories
7 g protein/2 g fat/28 g carbohydrates

Peel onion, chop finely, and purée along with garbanzos and any liquid from the garbanzo bean can. If necessary, add 1 tablespoon water or vegetable stock. Peel garlic, chop finely, and add to garbanzo purée along with spices, lemon juice, parsley, and egg. Mix ingredients thoroughly. Moisten your hands and shape mixture into balls about 1$\frac{1}{2}$ inches in diameter.

In a deep-fryer, heat oil to 350°F and fry falafel in batches for 3–4 minutes until crispy. Remove and drain on paper towels.

Falafel are delicious with a yogurt-cucumber sauce seasoned with cumin and cilantro.

Deep-Fried Bean Fritters

The base for these bean appetizers is not very firm so you have to slide them into the hot oil very slowly to allow them to keep their shape.

Serves 4:
¼ cup black-eyed peas
¼ medium onion
½ red bell pepper
½ cup cornstarch
1 egg white
Salt (preferably kosher or sea)
Freshly ground cayenne pepper
Plus:
Vegetable oil for deep-frying

Prep time: 35 minutes
Per serving approx: 113 calories
2 g protein/4 g fat/19 g carbohydrates

Soak peas in water overnight. Drain and rub between your hands to remove skins. In a blender, mix peas with 3 tablespoons water to make a fine purée. Peel onion and chop finely. Remove stem, seeds, and ribs from bell pepper and dice finely. Mix onion, bell pepper, cornstarch, and egg white into pea purée and season generously with salt, pepper, and cayenne.

In a deep-fryer, heat oil to 325°F. Using 2 teaspoons, carefully push small portions of the pea mixture into the hot oil. Deep-fry and stir for 5 minutes until crispy, then remove and drain on paper towels.

In their native Nigeria, these bean appetizers are known as "akara." You might serve them with a sweet and spicy chili sauce if you and your guests are looking for a dip.

These refined, tasty sandwiches are best with a spicy dip. They go especially well with a sweet and spicy Chinese chili sauce or light soy sauce.

Serves 6:
9 ounces scallops
1 clove garlic
1 teaspoon fresh ginger
4–5 scallions
1 red chili pepper
9 ounces ground pork
Juice from ½ kaffir lime
Lime zest
1 egg
Freshly ground black pepper
Salt (preferably kosher or sea)
Light soy sauce
1 teaspoon chopped cilantro
4 slices white bread, about ¼-inch thick
Plus:
4 tablespoons olive oil
Lettuce leaves for garnish

Prep time: 45 minutes
Per serving approx: 300 calories
17 g protein/20 g fat/13 g carbohydrates

Clean scallops, removing muscle if necessary, and dice into pieces of about ¼ inch. Peel garlic and ginger and chop both very finely. Clean scallions and chop finely. Cut chili pepper in half, remove stem, seeds, and ribs, and dice finely.

In a bowl, mix scallops, garlic, ginger, scallions, chili pepper, ground pork, lime juice, lime peel, egg, pepper, salt, soy sauce, and cilantro. Distribute mixture evenly on bread slices and spread smooth.

In a pan, heat olive oil, add open-faced sandwiches and starting with the meat side down, fry over moderate heat for about 15 minutes. Then turn and fry on the bread side for another 2 minutes. Remove sandwiches from the pan and cut in half diagonally. Garnish with various types of lettuce leaves. Be sure to serve sandwiches nice and hot—that's how they taste best.

The fine aroma of the scallops and seasonings is best enjoyed when served fresh from the pan.

Mussels with Bell Pepper Garni

The fresher the mussel, the better the flavor! This recipe from Spain uses Galician mussels, among the finest in the world. Their flesh has an especially mild flavor and a bright orange color.

Serves 2:
2¼ pounds mussels, in the shell
⅔ cup dry white wine
2 bay leaves
12 black peppercorns
2 teaspoons lemon juice
Salt (preferably kosher or sea)
Freshly ground white pepper
For the bell pepper mixture:
1 each small green and red bell pepper
¼ cup shallots, chopped finely
1 tablespoon extra virgin olive oil
Salt (preferably kosher or sea)
Freshly ground white pepper

Prep time: 40 minutes
Per serving approx: 50 calories
6 g protein/2 g fat/16 g carbohydrates

Braise diced bell peppers with sautéed shallots over medium heat while stirring constantly. Add seasoning.

Place mussels in the shells and cover each with a spoonful of the hot bell pepper and shallot mixture. Serve immediately.

Scrub mussels with a brush under cold running water. Throw away any that are open and pull off the beards with your fingers. Place mussels in a pot with wine, bay leaves, and peppercorns, cover, and steam 5–6 minutes until the mussels have opened. Throw away any that are still closed because these are most likely spoiled. Line a colander with a kitchen towel or cheesecloth and pour the mussel stock through it. Season stock with lemon juice and, if necessary, salt and pepper, and reduce to 4–5 tablespoons.

For the bell pepper mixture, cut peppers in half, remove seeds and ribs, and dice very finely. Heat oil and saute shallots over medium heat until tender. Add 1 tablespoon mussel stock and reduce. Add diced bell peppers and braise until tender while stirring constantly, as described in the first picture above. Pour remaining mussel stock over diced bell peppers and simmer for several minutes.

Open mussels all the way and throw away one half of each shell. Place mussel in the other half and continue as described in the second picture.

The bell pepper mixture makes a delicious topping for the delicate mussel meat. Served in its own shell, this sophisticated tidbit is a delicious Mediterranean starter.

Lamb Chops with Salsa

Meat from young lambs is very popular because it's so tender and extremely tasty. These chops are especially juicy when left on the bone. Though they should be fried only very briefly, the temperature must be very high. They taste fantastic with the fiery hot salsa.

Serves 6:
12 lamb chops, Frenched (2–3 ounces each)
Salt (preferably kosher or sea)
Freshly ground black pepper
2 tablespoons olive oil

For the marinade:
1 clove garlic
1 red chili pepper
1 tablespoon chopped rosemary
1 tablespoon chopped parsley
1 tablespoon chopped thyme
Zest and juice from 1 lemon
3 tablespoons olive oil

For the salsa:
3–4 beefsteak tomatoes
¼ medium onion
1–2 cloves garlic
½ red bell pepper
3 chipotle peppers or 2 small fresh chili peppers
2 tablespoons tomato paste
¼ cup vegetable stock
2 tablespoons chopped parsley
1 pinch sugar
Salt (preferably kosher or sea)
Freshly ground black pepper

Prep time: 1 hour
Per serving approx: 337 calories
25 g protein/22 g fat/10 g carbohydrates

For the marinade, peel garlic and chop finely. Rinse chili pepper, remove stem and seeds, and cut into rings. Combine chopped garlic, chili rings, herbs, lemon peel, and oil.

Season lamb chops with salt and pepper, place in a shallow, flat bottom bowl or lasagna dish, and drizzle with marinade.

For the salsa, blanch tomatoes for 15 seconds in boiling water, remove peels, cut into quarters, remove cores and seeds, and chop coarsely. Peel onions and garlic and chop. Rinse bell pepper, peel, remove stems and seeds, and dice finely. Drain chipotles and dice finely. Place all these ingredients in a pot. Stir in tomato paste and stock, add parsley, and season with sugar, salt, and pepper. Bring to a boil and reduce over low heat for 10–15 minutes, stirring occasionally. Let salsa cool.

Heat oil and sauté lamb chops on both sides for 1–2 minutes. Remove, arrange on a platter, and serve with the salsa on the side.

Under the Japanese name "tofu," this versatile, soybean byproduct has achieved fame far beyond the boundaries of Asia. Many types are available, characterized by different seasonings and consistencies. You can buy tofu in well-stocked grocery stores or in Asian markets. Tofu should be refrigerated and kept in water that is changed daily.

Serves 4:
1 cup medium-firm tofu
1 tablespoon finely diced carrot
1 tablespoon finely diced leek
1 finely chopped scallion
1 tablespoon chopped herbs
(parsley, chives)
1 egg
½ cup wheat flour
Salt (preferably kosher or sea)
Freshly ground black pepper
For the bell pepper dip:
1 roasted bell pepper, cleaned
1 tablespoon diced onion

4 tablespoons olive oil
2 tablespoons white wine vinegar
6 tablespoons vegetable stock
Salt (preferably kosher or sea)
Freshly ground black pepper
1 tablespoon chopped parsley
Plus:
3 tablespoons vegetable oil for frying
Toothpicks
Italian parsley leaves

Prep time: 35 minutes
Per serving approx: 258 calories
8 g protein/18 g fat/17 g carbohydrates

First prepare the dip. Chop roasted peppers finely. Peel onions and chop finely. In a sauté pan, heat oil and sauté chopped bell peppers and onions without browning. Pour in vinegar and vegetable stock and remove from heat. Season with salt and pepper, stir in parsley, and let sauce cool until lukewarm.

Pat tofu dry and mash finely with a fork. Mix with carrots, leek, scallions, and herbs. Add egg and flour, season with salt and pepper, and knead with your hands into a dough. If it's too soft, work in a little more flour.

From the tofu dough, make 14–18 cakes. Heat oil and sauté cakes over medium heat for 2–3 minutes on each side.

Arrange tofu cakes on a platter, pierce with toothpicks and garnish with parsley leaves. Serve bell pepper dip on the side.

Tofu cakes with vegetables and herbs make a healthy snack. They can be served with a colorful, light, bell pepper sauce as a dip.

Almonds 12
Anchovies
    baguette niçoise 54
    golden-fried cod 92
    prosciutto-wrapped
        polenta 102
Asparagus 30

Bacon
    deep-fried cheese
        pockets 74
    puff pastry meat
        pockets 80
Bamboo shoots 90
Beans, garbanzo 114
Beef
    Keftédes 110
    puff pastry meat
        pockets 80
Bread
    baguette niçoise 54
    bell pepper-tuna crostini 48
    canapés 30
    crostini with chicken livers 50
    feta with herbs on
        tomatoes 52
    filled pumpernickel 42
    hot sandwiches with
        scallops 118

Camembert
    cheese cubes with red
        currant sauce 104
    petits fours with cheese 36
Cashews 12
Chicken
    chicken wontons 90
    skewered chicken
        croquettes 108
    skewered chicken
        meatballs 106
Chicken livers 50
Cod 92
Crabmeat 58

Crackers
    colorful cracker
        assortment 24
    cracker canapés with
        mushroom cream 22
    three cheese crackers 44
Cream cheese 46
Currants 104

Feta 52
Figs 26

Gouda
    assorted skewers 10
    cheese spirals 86
    three cheese crackers 44
Gruyere
    salami & cheese cream
        puffs 20
    three cheese rolls 88

Ham 94
Hazelnuts 12

Lamb
    lamb chops with salsa 122
    samosas 72
Lemon grass
    shrimp on lemon grass
        skewers 70
    skewered chicken
        meatballs 106

Masa harina 82
Mascarpone
    puff pastry squares
        with cheese filling 40
    stuffed figs 26
Mozzarella
    deep-fried cheese
        pockets 74
    Mozzarella skewers 28
    pork patties au gratin 98
Mushrooms, shiitake 90

Mushrooms, white
    cracker canapés with
        mushroom cream 22
    two cheese stuffed
        vegetables 38
Mussels 120

Olives
    baguette niçoise 54
    Involtini di Vitello   94

Parmesan 88
Peas, black-eyed 116
Peppers, bell
    bell pepper-tuna crostini 48
    chicken wontons 90
    mini pizzas 84
    mussels with bell
        pepper garni 120
    skewered chicken
        croquettes 108
    tofu cakes 124
    Tuscan pork skewers 96
Phyllo 58
Polenta 102
Pork
    Asian pork hedgehogs 112
    hot sandwiches with
        scallops 118
    Keftédes 110
    pork patties au gratin 98
    puff pastry meat pockets 80
    skewered chicken
        croquettes 108
    Tuscan pork skewers 96
    wonton-style stuffed
        shrimp 76
Prosciutto
    grissini with ham 14
    petits fours with cheese 36
    prosciutto-wrapped
        polenta 102
    stuffed figs 26
    three cheese rolls 88

Puff Pastry
    cheese spirals 86
    palmiers 18
    Parmesan twists 14
    puff pastry meat pockets 80
    puff pastry squares with
        cheese filling 40

Quark
    colorful cracker
        assortment 24
    petits fours with cheese 36
    two cheese stuffed
        vegetables 38

Rice, sushi
    Asian pork hedgehogs 112
    maki sushi with wild rice
        and tofu 66
    nigiri sushi with shrimp 64
    nigiri sushi with tuna 62
Rice, wild 66
Ricotta
    colorful cracker
        assortment 24
    deep-fried cheese
        pockets 74
    petits fours with cheese 36
Ricotta dumplings 34
    salmon canapés 32
    three cheese crackers 44
    three cheese rolls 88
    two cheese stuffed
        vegetables 38
Roquefort
    Roquefort cookies 16
    three cheese crackers 44

Salami
    assorted skewers 10
    mini pizzas 84
    palmiers 18
    salami & cheese cream
        puffs 20
    salami skewers 56
Salmon, smoked 32
Sausage, veal liver 42
Scallops 118
Shrimp
    nigiri sushi with shrimp 64
    phyllo cups 58
    prawn rolls 78
    seafood skewers 100
    shrimp empanadas 82
    shrimp on lemon grass
        skewers 70
    wonton-style stuffed
        shrimp 76
Spring roll wrappers
    chicken wontons 90
    three cheese rolls 88
    wonton-style stuffed
        shrimp 76
Squid 100
Stilton 36

Tilsiter 42
Tofu
    maki sushi with wild rice
        and tofu 66
    tofu cakes 124

Tomatoes
    assorted skewers 10
    Canapés 30
    feta with herbs on
        tomatoes 52
    lamb chops with salsa 122
    mini pizzas 84
    Mozzarella skewers 28
    prosciutto-wrapped
        polenta 102
    seafood skewers 100
    shrimp empanadas 82
    stuffed tomatoes 46
    two cheese stuffed
        vegetables 38
    Tuscan pork skewers 96
Trout
    Canapés 30
Tuna
    bell pepper-tuna crostini 48
    nigiri sushi with tuna 62

Veal 94

Walnuts 12

Yogurt 72

Zucchini 96